COMPOSITION
Writing, Revising, and Speaking

Virginia Tech First-Year Composition Faculty Authors

Robin Allnutt
Jennifer Barton
Lissa Bloomer
Sheila Carter-Tod
Leigh Corrigan
Michael Dimmick
Katie Fallon
Kathryn Graham
Paul Heilker
Bob Hicok
Cathy Hudgins
Julia Johnson
Shoshana Knapp
Jennifer Lawrence
Victoria LeCorre
Lisa Leslie
Alice LoMascolo
Julie Mengert
Nancy Metz
Shawn Mole
Lynette Moyer
Aileen Murphy
Steve Oakey

Mary Beth Pennington
Suzanne Reisinger
Michele Ren
Lucinda Roy
Cheryl Ruggiero
Sue Saffle
Emily Sewall
Robert Siegle
Michael Smith
Michael Squires
Phil Tietjen
Gyorgyi Voros
Bruce Watson
Ed Weathers
Dennis Welch

Managing Editors
Lissa Bloomer
Lisa Leslie

General Editors
Nancy Metz
Cheryl Ruggiero

ISBN 0-536-948542

2005240182

EM/JM

Please visit our web site at *www.pearsoncustom.com*

PEARSON CUSTOM PUBLISHING
75 Arlington Street, Suite 300, Boston, MA 02116
A Pearson Education Company

Table of Contents

Acknowledgements

The English Department would like to acknowledge and give special thanks to Virginia Tech alumnus Richard Mallory Allnutt, seen here as photographed by Alexia Marie Garamfalvi, for the beautiful photographs featured on the front and back covers, as well as the beginning of Chapter 2, of this textbook. Richard received part of his undergraduate education here at Virginia Tech, left us for Leicester University in England, then later returned to Tech for his MSc and PhD in Electrical Engineering. Richard now serves as both an Engineering Consultant by designing components for spacecraft antennae and as a freelance photographer. His photos are on covers of magazines such as *JazzTimes* and *Swing Journal*, and in a variety of inter-

Richard M. Allnutt

national aviation magazines such as *Flypast, Aeroplane, Aircraft Illustrated, Combat Aircraft* and even the New Zealand journal *Classic Wings*. Richard also was the set photographer for the feature film *The Distance*, has shot promotional photography for Concord Records and HBO's *The Wire*, and was the production printer for *The Art in War* — a nationally acclaimed photography show on the war in Iraq. More of Richard's work can be viewed at http://www.rmallnutt.com. Thank you, Richard!

The Editors and the Editorial Board would like to acknowledge the hard work of the Virginia Tech composition faculty and the Newman Library Instructional Staff in the production of this book. We are especially grateful to Aileen Murphy for her photo expertise and for providing the photographs of students and their teachers. Suzanne Reisinger, Mike Smith, Jennifer Lawrence, Leigh Corrigan, and Serena Frost read stacks of student essays to select the ones appearing in this year's book, and Michael Honchock heroically photocopied and kept track of them all. Monique Dufour wrote our section in the University Common Book. Ada Hatzios of Virginia Tech Photographic Services provided us with assistance in our original selection of images from the Virginia Tech Photo Archive. Producing this book has been a marvelous collaborative effort, involving the writing, editing, energy, and ideas of a diverse group of talented people, including — in addition to the authors and editors listed on our title page — the following contributors over the several years of the project: Nicole Auer, Jennifer Bolton, Eva Brumberger, Teggin Chamberlain, Cathee Dennison, Jim Dubinsky, David Griffith, Donald Hall, JoAnn Harvill, Christine Hughes, Michele James-Deramo, Steve Kark, Alice Kinder, Sean Kotz, Emily Sewall, Stephanie Martin, Sue McGann-Osborn, Mary Denson Moore, Leslie Neilan, Marie Paretti, Nancy Jurek, Dave Rutkowski, John Stubbs, Karen Swenson, Tyra Twomey, and Marc Zaldivar.

A Note on the Text

This composition text is a writing project that teachers in Virginia Tech's composition program assigned themselves. We generated its ideas in noisy workshops. We shared our experiences as teachers — successes and failures. We had to explain to each other what we really meant when we talked about "good writing," and we had to produce examples of our students' work to be judged by others. Our debates challenged us to articulate our own positions with the thoughtfulness, clarity, and coherence we expect of you, our students. And, as we urge you to do in the chapter on Spoken Composition, we had to become active listeners.

Cheryl Ruggiero and Nancy Metz

Nearly every member of our composition faculty participated in the discussions that gave rise to this book. Students gave us written feedback. Paul Heilker, in close collaboration with Pearson Custom Publishing, provided leadership, expertise, and heroic late-night labors to get the first versions of the book off the ground. Approximately forty faculty members drafted revisions last year and this year. An Editorial Board composed of Robin Allnutt, Jennifer Barton, Julie Mengert, Suzanne Reisinger, Lucinda Roy, Michael Smith, and Ed Weathers made design decisions and reviewed drafts.

Managing Editors Lissa Bloomer and Lisa Leslie coordinated the work of the many faculty and student authors. As General Editors, we brought the pieces together into a coherent whole, editing the text so that the voices of forty writers sound like one. Like the assignments you will be completing in First-Year Composition, we felt the pressure of our deadline, yet even as this finished manuscript goes to press, we are thinking of the next version. You can help by letting us know what works for you and what else you need from the text.

Our journey from reflection, discussion, and debate to drafting, revision, and design has been challenging but also gratifying, even joyous. We wish you the same rewarding journey as you make your way through this book!

—Nancy Metz and Cheryl Ruggiero
General Editors

Welcome!

This textbook was designed for your studies at Virginia Tech. Developed in partnership with a leading publisher, it brings together material from three sources:

Shelli Fowler, Cheryl Ruggiero,
Sheila Carter-Tod, and Paul Heilker

- chapters written specifically for our courses by Virginia Tech English faculty
- papers written by Virginia Tech First-Year Composition students
- advice on writing by Virginia Tech faculty and administrators

It is a unique and growing book, and we ask for your feedback to improve it in its next edition. Let your instructor know at any time what works and doesn't work for you; at the end of the semester, your instructor will provide a survey for your reactions and advice.

We invite you to open our book with an acknowledgement and a promise. *We acknowledge that composition is hard work. We promise to do all we can to support you in this work.* We urge you to take advantage of many avenues of assistance we offer:

- Actively connect with the material in this book.

- Talk with your teacher during office hours.

- Work with the expert consultants in the Writing Center: Shanks 340, 231-5436.

- Know that our doors are always open to you when you have questions.

—The First-Year Composition Team

Paul Heilker
Director, Composition 1994 – 2004
Founding editor

Shelli Fowler
Director, Graduate Education
Development Institute
Interim Director, Composition
2004 – 2005

Sheila Carter-Tod
Associate Director, Composition

Cheryl Ruggiero
Assistant Director, Composition

"Writing is thinking."

Charles Steger
President of Virginia Tech

Message from the Chair

Types of Writers (Most of Them—Alas —A Lot Like Yours Truly)

A Note from Lucinda Roy, Chair of English

Commanding a student to write on demand is like handing a patient a cup in a doctor's office—it's often excruciatingly difficult to perform well. Those of us who are Physicians of Language understand this. We are sympathetic. We too struggle to express ourselves; we too often fall short.

After teaching for more than twenty-five years, I've learned that there are many different approaches taken by beginning writers as they face the horrors of the Blank Page. Each approach is fascinating in its own way; each one tells us something about the nature of fear. When we are commanded to write something, we are often incapable of writing anything meaningful. Instead, we become parodies of ourselves—cartoon characters who speak and write in ways we'd normally be ashamed to do in public.

There's the student—call him Monty—who enters the realm of the essay the way other people enter a theme park. Excited to the point of irresponsibility, Monty hurtles through the space of the page like a thing possessed. He writes he knows not what, but he writes with vigor. Thrilled by his own use of the unfamiliar words he discovers when he goes on a rampage through his tattered thesaurus, Monty employs phrases like "*totally* awesome," as if the state of awesomeness were somehow relative. He doesn't re-read what he's written; there's no time. Stopping is dangerous. The only possible way to complete the paper he never wanted to write in the first place is by resorting to recklessness. If he ends up bloody in the last paragraph, at least he'll be able to turn the thing in and never have to think about it again. When I'm being this student, I'm happy with my C. C isn't a bad grade. Better than D—far, *far* better than F. Monty and I lurch onwards to the next essay unhampered by reflection, addicted to speed.

Then there's the student who begins a slow tap on the keyboard only to find herself enveloped in a kind of linguistic coma. For our purposes, her name is Looella. Dreamily waltzing through her essay on Whatever-Is-Abstract-and-Cannot-Be-Pinned-Down-in-Any-Concrete-Fashion, Looella (known to her friends as Looloo) glides over language as if it were an ice rink. Once in a while a hole opens up in the middle of a paragraph and swallows Looloo whole. Sputtering but undaunted, she flings herself back onto the white page, struggles to an upright position, and resumes her frigid pirouettes. Page 5 is just beyond that next pirouette in her three-point enumeration essay — see it there? All she and I have to do is skim over the surface of things, avoid the hard questions; all we have to do is keep our eyes just slightly out of focus.

And then there's the student, Mikey, who plans to get to his paper as soon as he's finished playing *Doom,* clipping his toenails, having a quick smoke, taking the dog for a walk, hanging out at the student union, and applying a touch of Rogaine. He knows that there are always better things to do than to write a paper for his first-year writing teacher. Why, only yesterday, he presented a forged note to his teacher (who says he can't write well?) and managed to get an extension on his first paper due to the untimely death of his great-aunt, a woman prone to resurrection. Yesterday, when he was seeing if he could catch the light in a state of repose when he opened and closed the refrigerator door, Mikey noted that, when he whistled, he could sometimes manage to make a chord — two notes at once — if not in harmony, then certainly a thing worthy of further investigation. Had Mikey worked on his essay, as he explained to his frazzled mother when she called him later that night, he'd have missed this whistling phenomenon altogether. "There's a chance I could be on *Letterman* if I practice," he tells her. Mikey and I are skilled in a manipulative kind of way. Sometimes we manage to avoid writing altogether. "Lying is an art," we tell each other. "An art we're very good at," we say smugly, ending in a preposition.

Then there's the poor student, Cindy, who believes that, as long as she writes in an elevated tone, she'll be persuasive. She too uses words she's never met before, but only if they are polysyllabic and hard to pronounce. She believes that, when you write, it's like being on a soap opera: nothing should remind you of real life. Modifiers, nouns, verbs — most of them should be the kind you rarely, if ever, use. Clichés are in for this particular student; they were never out, in fact, because they are abidingly true, which is what made them clichés in the first place. She tries to explain this to her teacher, but her teacher is hard-hearted and a Pisces, and therefore doesn't understand. A typical sentence authored by this student goes something like this: "In my heart of hearts I know that there are fallopian errors out there all over the place; in fact, the miasma of origination interrogates us to strive harder for expressionism lest we cast our pearls to swine." She and I read our own words with a passion that borders on fanaticism. We are zealots of high-falutin' phraseology. Our butchery of the language is so imprecise it can make your eyes water.

Last, there's the student-writer, LeRoy, who gets on everyone's nerves by producing something quite wonderful every time he picks up a pen or turns on his laptop. Infuriatingly good, he makes the rest of us look bad. He hands things in on time, rarely makes a spelling blunder, and generally ingratiates himself into subjects that seem to us to be impossibly impenetrable. How can you write an interesting essay on colitis, for example? A nasty disease that he, nevertheless, managed to turn into something so wonderful it seemed to rise up off the page and fly. LeRoy drives us nuts.

So what do you do if you're not naturally good with words? What do you do if, when you speak, your tongue ties itself up like a pretzel and turns you into a source of ridicule? I'm not sure I know the answer to this because I myself am guilty of every one of these flawed approaches. I stutter when I'm nervous; I've thrown away literally thousands of pages I once thought were brilliant—a view shared by both me and my mother simultaneously. But, at last, bruised and battered, I decided to adopt a kind of creed when it comes to writing-on-demand.

1. I write about things I care about.
2. I listen to myself as I write and speak, forcing myself to change voices when I begin to sound like a distant relative who doesn't know me very well.
3. I ask for help from teachers; I look for help from texts.
4. I'm not ashamed when I get something wrong or employ some malapropism that others find amusing (or are forced to look up).
5. I refuse to be intimidated by words; I refuse to let them defeat me; I refuse to be afraid of semicolons.
6. I persuade myself that what I'm about to write could mean something.
7. I remember that language makes love to the senses, to the intellect, to reason, and to passion.
8. I read and re-read and read again, honing what I've said, listening carefully to the words of others, accepting the fact that language can never be more than approximation.
9. I don't flog a horse suffering from five-day rigor mortis. If the subject is dead, it's dead. I choose another one. Trying to breathe life into dead things is both futile and unhealthy.
10. I write to learn even as I learn to write. Discovery and communication lie at the heart of composition. When we write and speak well, we can be recognized at last for who we are; it's how we wave to each other across the expanse of the silent page.

I am the Chair of English, but I cannot teach you how to write. What we hope to do as teachers is to take you to a place where writing is possible, a place where you feel empowered to speak. We hope to guide you to a location where thought without reflection has no allure, where all the words you speak and all the words you read come back to you in new and wondrous configurations.

There is so much sorrow and so much glory around us. Discovering it through language is the gift we hope you'll share with us.

Writing is hard; silence is worse. In the year 2005, it's still possible to say something of significance. It's time for our words to grow wings.

—Lucinda Roy, *Chair, Department of English*
April 2005

Virginia Tech
First-Year Composition
Program Overview

1.1 ■ Course Themes and Options in First-Year Composition

■ *Themes*

In each section of first-year composition, texts and discussions focus on one of these themes:

◆ **Writing Through the Environment:** In this course, students examine human perspectives on the environment and human relationships with the nonhuman world. They read, discuss, and write about a variety of texts that explore the ways language and culture have shaped and continue to shape our conceptions of nature.

◆ **Writing Through Cross-Cultural Contact:** In this course, students explore how culture makes us who we are and what happens when we encounter people whose culture differs from our own. Students examine the diversity, richness, and beauty of cross-cultural contact — and the problems that cross-cultural contact can cause.

◆ **Writing Through Science and Technology:** In this course, students explore the problems, delights, and challenges created by recent developments in science and technology. The course examines various topics, such as cloning, genetic engineering, and the impact of computers on people's lives and on traditional concepts of intellectual property.

◆ **Writing Through Arts and Aesthetics:** In this course, students focus on aesthetic questions. How do we respond to art? How do human beings create art? Students explore the territories of art — in the past and in the present — and they look at the many ways art comforts the afflicted and afflicts the comfortable.

◆ **Writing Through the University Experience:** In this course, students explore the University itself as a text, one filled with energy, ideas, choices, conflicts, and obstacles. Students critically examine this complex text while they work toward a clearer sense of why they are here, what they want, and how best to achieve their goals.

3

■ *The Service-Learning Option*
http://www.majbill.vt.edu/sl

Some sections of first-year composition courses give students the opportunity to participate in service-learning, which integrates community service with classroom instruction. Service-learning allows students to meet real community needs and to experience firsthand what it means to contribute to community life. To paraphrase the Virginia Tech motto, service-learning puts knowledge to work for the community.

1.2 ■ Learning Objectives in First-Year Composition

By the time you finish the first-year composition sequence, you will be able to do the following:

Critical Reading
- read closely a variety of texts
- locate and articulate values and assumptions underlying your own opinions and those of other writers

Critical Thinking
- discover patterns of information within and across fields of data
- interpret the meaning(s) of those patterns of information
- argue convincingly for the significance of your interpretation(s)

Writing Process
- propose writing projects
- use effective invention, planning, and drafting strategies
- revise at whole-text and paragraph levels
- edit at the sentence level for clear, concise diction and syntax

Analytical Writing
- create focused, effective thesis statements
- construct focused, coherent, well-supported essays
- construct focused paragraphs unified by one main idea
- use evidence to make both an immediate point (in a paragraph, for example) and a larger point that supports the essay's thesis
- organize information into patterns that consciously and deliberately serve the goals of the document

1

◆ use transitions effectively (between sentences and between paragraphs)

Research-Based Writing

◆ accurately summarize source material

◆ locate and correctly cite authoritative sources to support assertions

◆ integrate this material smoothly into the argument

◆ use outside material without detracting from your own independent point of view

Grammar and Mechanics

◆ produce a finished, formal document that contains on average no more than one grammatical, mechanical, punctuation, or spelling error per page

Oral Competency

◆ make group and individual oral presentations (spoken compositions) that offer focused, coherent, developed content and engage the audience through effective eye contact, purposeful stance, meaningful gestures, and appropriate speed and volume of delivery

Digital Literacy

◆ produce effective formal e-mail and evaluate the quality of online sources of information

1.3 ▌ The Assignment Sequence in First-Year Composition

As you work through the following sequence of increasingly complex assignments, you will develop abilities in all the above areas, and you will become more confident as both a writer and a speaker. Our assignment sequence emphasizes *analysis* because most of the writing you will do in college will be analytical writing.

To analyze something is to break it down into its component parts in order to discover how those parts work together to produce the whole. This process requires both *perception* and *conception*: first we *perceive* a pattern within or across a set of data; then we *conceive* of what that pattern means. By discovering a meaningful pattern or structure within the data and explaining this meaning to others, we turn mere data into potentially useful information.

The assignment sequences in ENGL 1105 and 1106/H1204 are carefully designed to help you learn how to do increasingly complex kinds of analysis. You will begin each course by working with one relatively simple text; then you will work with two more complex texts; finally, you will work with an array of complex texts. Thus, you will progress from analyzing single sets of data, to analyzing two sets, to analyzing more than two.

Papers in Sequence	Name	Source Texts
#1 — 1105	Analysis I	1 short text
#2 — 1105	Synthesis	2 short texts
#3 — 1105	Position	3 or more short texts
#4 — 1106/H1204	Analysis II	1 long text
#5 — 1106/H1204	Contextualized Analysis	1 long text, 1 short text
#6 — 1106/H1204	Research Paper	multiple texts

1.4 ■ Summary of Requirements: ENGL 1105, ENGL 1106/H1204

In English 1105 you will submit a minimum of 15 pages of formal graded writing; in English 1106/H1204, you will submit a minimum of 20 pages of formal graded writing. In each course you will also submit a minimum of 20 pages of informal writing, such as journals, reader responses, electronic bulletin board postings, chat room interchanges, and so on; this informal writing will not necessarily be formally evaluated. You will also give one group and one individual oral presentation in each course.

You will also be required to complete the *Grammar Gym* (our online, self-paced grammar tutorial) with a score of 85% or better before turning in your second formal paper. The Grammar Gym is accessible via the English Department homepage (http://www.english.vt.edu/%7EIDLE/Gym2/). Writing Center tutors are available for anyone needing help with the Grammar Gym.

■ ENGL 1105 Requirements

Essay 1: Analysis I

Overall Goal: to learn the techniques of detailed critical analysis through examination of a single short text

General Assignment: Explore the relationship between a single text (a short set of poems, a short story, a short novel or drama, or a short work of nonfiction) and some aspect of the course theme.

Essay 2: Synthesis

Overall Goal: to learn to comprehend, evaluate, and synthesize the ideas of writers who have explored the course theme

General Assignment: Write an essay in which you synthesize 2 texts relevant to the course theme.

Essay 3: Position

Overall Goal: to learn how to develop a detailed, coherent, well-supported argument using several sources

General Assignment: Using the readings this semester and your own experiences, develop and defend a position on a key issue pertinent to the course theme.

Oral Presentations (Spoken Compositions)

Overall Goal: to meet the National Communication Association standards for effective oral discourse for college sophomores

General Assignment: Participate in two oral presentations—

- one group presentation, with 4–6 students speaking for a total of 12–15 minutes
- one individual presentation of 5 minutes

Grammar Gym

Overall Goal: to meet college-level standards for grammatical correctness

General Assignment: Complete the online Grammar Gym tutorial and pass all four tests with a score of 85% or better on each.

Reflection

Overall Goal: to develop as an independent learner and prepare for creating academic and professional portfolios

General Assignment: Write reflectively in a variety of contexts as indicated by your instructor (see section 1.6).

■ *ENGL 1106/H1204 Requirements*

Essay 4: Analysis II

Overall Goal: to refine and extend analytical proficiency through examination of a single long text

General Assignment: Explore the relationship between a single text (an extensive set of poems, a full-length novel or drama, or a book-length work of nonfiction) and the larger issues of the course.

Essay 5: Contextualized Analysis

Overall Goal: to ground a critical analysis in a larger context and set it against the work of other writers

General Assignment: Explore the relationship between a particular text (an extensive set of poems, a full-length novel or drama, or a book-length work of nonfiction) and some aspect of the course theme, using at least one additional text to ground that relationship.

Essay 6: The Research Paper

The Research Paper is the capstone assignment for the First-Year Composition Program. It will thus draw upon everything you have learned in ENGL 1105/1106/H1204. The Research Paper is a research-based writing project with four parts:

A. Required Information Literacy Unit

B. Research Question and Annotated Bibliography

C. Paper Proposal

D. Research Paper

Overall Goal: to research a topic of your own choosing related to your readings in the course, to evaluate the fruits of your research, to develop an original thesis based on your research, and to weave outside sources into your writing to create a focused, coherent, convincing argument

General Assignment: Write a 2100–3000 word (7–10 pages of your own text, exclusive of cover, graphics, extensive block quotations, and Works Cited pages) thesis-driven research paper developed in response to course readings. Your instructor may require that at least one course text be part of the subject matter of the paper. At least four (4) outside sources in addition to any course text(s) must be used; individual instructors may require more sources.

Oral Presentations (Spoken Compositions)

Overall Goal: to meet the National Communication Association standard for effective oral discourse for college sophomores

General Assignment: Participate in two oral presentations—

◆ one group presentation, with 4–6 students speaking for a total of 12–15 minutes

◆ one individual presentation of 5 minutes

Grammar Gym

(in 1106/1204, applicable only to students who placed out of 1105)

Overall Goal: to meet college-level standards for grammatical correctness

General Assignment: Complete the online Grammar Gym tutorial and pass all four tests with a score of 85% or better on each.

Reflection

Overall Goal: to develop as an independent learner and to prepare for creating academic and professional portfolios

General Assignment: Write reflectively in a variety of contexts as indicated by your instructor (see section 1.6).

1.5 ■ Virginia Tech Standards for Grading

You may be wondering what your English instructors will be looking for when they grade your essays. Listed below are some basic grading criteria. Keep in mind, though, that good writing cannot be reduced to a universally applicable set of characteristics. Good writers sometimes break the rules, making deliberate — and effective — use of contradictions, abrupt transitions, and even sentence fragments. Still, the criteria listed below provide a helpful overview of Virginia Tech standards for essay grading, standards applicable to most essays and assignments. Since most students come to Virginia Tech as competent writers, we begin with the characteristics of the C paper.

Characteristics of the satisfactory or C paper. The competent paper demonstrates the following:

Focus: The paper has a clear thesis. The thesis may be general or obvious, but it serves as a focus for the paper.

Organization/Development: The paper is organized clearly — the reader can follow the ideas easily. Some details are included, but support for generalizations could be stronger or more strategic. Individual paragraphs are unified and coherent.

Style: The prose is readable. Transitions between sentences and paragraphs are generally clear.

Mechanics: The paper is relatively free of grammar, punctuation, spelling, and other errors.

Research (if applicable): The paper integrates outside sources well and cites sources accurately.

Characteristics of a good or B paper. The good paper demonstrates the following:

Focus: The paper has a clear, compelling thesis.

Organization/Development: The paper is clearly organized and focused. It provides adequate support for the thesis with specific details. Individual paragraphs are generally well developed and well organized.

Style: The prose is crisp, concise, precise, and readable, with few clichés. Sentence structure is appropriately varied and complex.

Mechanics: The paper has only a few minor grammatical problems; these problems do not interfere with comprehension.

Research (if applicable): The paper employs and integrates outside sources in sophisticated ways. All sources are properly documented.

Characteristics of an excellent or A paper. The excellent paper demonstrates the following:

Focus: The paper has a sophisticated, compelling thesis.

Organization/Development: The paper is sharply focused and the material is organized for maximum clarity and impact. The thesis is supported by a detailed, coherent, in-depth argument. Individual paragraphs are likewise focused, coherent, and fully developed.

Style: The prose is not merely precise, concise, and readable, but it is also fluid and graceful.

Mechanics: The paper has few — if any — grammatical errors.

Research (if applicable): The paper synthesizes well-chosen and well-digested resources with the student's own ideas, producing an original and sophisticated piece of analysis. All sources are properly documented.

Characteristics of an unsatisfactory or D paper. The unsatisfactory paper suffers from the following problems:

Focus: A thesis can be identified, but it may lack clarity or focus.

Organization/Development: The paper is not clearly organized and provides very little supporting evidence.

Style: The prose is wordy, imprecise, and suffers from poor word choice and awkward, often incorrect, sentence structure. Transitions between sentences and between paragraphs are often vague or lacking entirely.

Mechanics: The paper contains many grammar and usage errors that interfere with comprehension.

Research (if applicable): The paper lacks coherence and depth and does not integrate sources smoothly into the argument. Sources are not properly cited and documented.

Characteristics of a failing or F paper. The failing paper fails in one or more of the following ways:

Focus: The paper lacks a thesis — it has only a topic, something to write about.

Organization/Development: The paper is not organized in any meaningful way, which is typical of papers that lack a strong thesis. Without a clear, specific point to prove, the writer simply cannot develop a focused, coherent, well-organized essay. Individual paragraphs are also disorganized and poorly developed.

Style: The prose suffers from wordiness, vagueness, poor word choice, faulty sentence structure, lack of transitions, etc.

Mechanics: The paper is marred by one grammatical error after another, making the paper very difficult to read.

Research (if applicable): The paper does not include sufficient sources for the topic, does not smoothly integrate sources, and does not properly cite and document sources. In the worst-case scenario, the writer intentionally plagiarizes.

1

1.6 ▌ The Reflection Component: Reflective Writing and Thinking in ENGL 1105 and 1106/H1204

One of the fundamental goals of the First-Year Composition Program is for you to become an independent learner — an independent thinker, writer, and speaker — someone who will be able to move into new academic, professional, and civic situations and continue to learn effectively by analyzing your thinking, writing, and speaking and adapting them to meet the new conditions.

Unfortunately, educational systems can sometimes give us more opportunities to remain dependent upon others for our learning than to become independent, offer us more incentive to remain passive receptors of knowledge than to become active participants in it, and be more interested in indoctrinating us in given ways of understanding and acting than in empowering us to develop our own ways.

Reflective thinking — *the ability to look at yourself, to examine your own state of mind, to critique your own knowledge, to analyze your own learning, thinking, writing, and speaking* — *is the key to your becoming an independent, active, empowered learner.* Reflection allows you to find personally meaningful connections across many disciplines and classroom contexts. Hence, reflective thinking is a fundamental component in a variety of teaching and learning initiatives here at Virginia Tech, including the Electronic Portfolio project.

Just as you look at your reflection in a mirror, reflective thinking asks you to look closely at yourself. You become the text you are analyzing. Writers engage in reflection in an effort to become self-monitoring, self-regulating, and self-directing, to gain control over the assumptions, values, concepts, and goals that drive their thinking, to become aware of the social, cultural, economic, and political lenses that determine their points of view and, ultimately, their actions.

Reflection is eminently practical because it allows you take responsibility for and control over your own development as a student, a professional, and a citizen, especially when you leave the controlled conditions of university learning. Reflection becomes critically important when you begin grappling with uncertainty, when problems have no answers or too many answers, when old ways of seeking solutions no longer work, when inherited, conventional wisdom from traditional authorities proves inadequate to the complexities at hand. The world of work and civic engagement beyond academia will regularly place you in such situations and reward those who are successful at reflection — that is, those who are self-monitoring, self-regulating, and self-directing.

Your instructor will ask you to engage in reflective thinking, speaking, and writing in a variety of ways throughout the semester, including but not limited to any or all of the following activities:

- discussion in class
- discussion in an online forum
- journal writing
- reading response writing
- informal in-class writing
- quizzes
- exams
- portfolio creation (electronic or paper)

You may be asked to reflect on your own experience with regard to the course theme, on your own writing, on your learning, and more. These reflections are a vital and required part of the course, and you will find them valuable to your future as well, as you begin to build an academic and then a professional portfolio.

Among questions you might find it helpful to address by the end of the semester, consider these:

- What have you learned about your learning preferences this semester?
- How might you take advantage of this awareness next semester?
- In what ways have you become a more independent learner this semester?
- What assumptions or values seemed to drive your thinking the most this semester?
- What are the strengths and weaknesses of working from these assumptions and values?
- How would you describe the point of view you employed most frequently this semester? What does this point of view help you see?
- What does this point of view prevent you from seeing?
- How did your opinion(s) or belief(s) change as a result of your experiences in this course?
- What have you learned about yourself as a writer or a speaker this semester?
- How might you employ this knowledge in the future?
- From which assignment did you learn the most?
- Why do you think this assignment worked especially well for you?
- How would you complete the following? This semester I focused on _____ because _____ .
- What personal goals are you setting based on your experience in this course?

1

Obviously, there are no right or wrong answers to any of these questions. What your instructor will want to see, and what you will also value, is that you have thought deeply about the questions, that you took care not to offer simplistic responses, but rather took the time and energy necessary to look carefully at yourself, analyze yourself, and render honest answers that do justice to your complexity as a person. In the end, remember that the audience for reflective thinking and writing is not your instructor, but you. Given a few cycles of such reflection, you will develop the kind of self-monitoring, self-regulating, and self-directing thinking and action that will define you as an independent learner, professional, and citizen, someone who controls his or her beliefs rather than being controlled by them.

1.7 The Common Book Project

We come to Virginia Tech from across the country and from down the road, each with our own stories, our own interests, dreams and plans. Across our differences, we have many things in common, including our Common Book.

The Common Book Project exists to create a space in which we can read and think together. Starting by reading the book as a community, we open a sustained conversation about the ideas and issues that the book raises. Over the course of your first year at Virginia Tech, you are invited not only to join this conversation, but to shape it with your questions and ideas.

Think of this book as a door into a world of ideas. It's a place where you belong, and that you help to create with your commitment to understanding ideas and issues as they matter to you. Reading the book is only the beginning. From this common starting point, we can then follow the questions where they may lead.

You might have the opportunity to work with the book in your classes and to discuss the issues that it raises from different majors and disciplines. You might have the opportunity to work with the book in your composition class. And you can participate in campus-wide events that will continue the conversation.

Yet the Common Book Project reminds us that we all can and do think beyond the classroom walls. We all have interests and passions that we pursue just because they matter to us. You might write stories or read for pleasure. You might play an instrument. You might take photographs or draw. So much of what we do best, we aren't required to do. The Common Book Project encourages and honors this extra-curricular intellectual and creative life.

Each spring, the Common Book Project publishes an online magazine, *The Commons*, in order to create a space in which you can share your ideas in public. *The Commons* publishes your work about the current Common Book and the issues that it raises, as well as work about your experience as a first-year student.

Visit www.commonbook.vt.edu for the current issue of *The Commons*, and for information about the Common Book Project, the current selection, and upcoming events.

— Monique Dufour
Coordinator, University Writing Program
Coordinator, University Common Book Program

Success Strategies in First-Year Composition

When I speak with employers, they indicate that, yes, technical knowledge is essential, but so are communication skills. Engineers can devise the most elegant and innovative solutions to technical problems, but if they cannot communicate these solutions to people they work for and with, then even the most wondrous solution is of little value.

—Bevlee A. Watford
Associate Dean for Academic Affairs,
College of Engineering

2

2.1 ■ Why Success Matters: Composition in the "Real World"

Our First-Year Composition courses will help you develop skills that are highly valued in the workplace, as well as at this university. Consider the following statistics from the Virginia Tech English Department website (www.english.vt.edu/comp1):

◆ College-educated workers spend, on average, 20 to 25% of their time writing. One study found that professional and technical employees spend 29% of their work time writing. An MIT study of the Exxon corporation found that engineers and intermediate managers spend 30% of their time writing, while supervisors spend 40% of their time writing.

◆ Ninety-six percent (96%) of Virginia Tech alumni report that writing is "important" or "very important" in their jobs. In a survey of engineers averaging 33 years on the job, 95% reported that their writing abilities are "very important or of critical importance in their positions."

◆ In one study, 89% of the respondents reported that "a person's need for writing ability increases as he or she is promoted." And in a survey of 245 engineers listed in *Engineers of Distinction*, 89% "reported that the ability to write is usually

2

an *important* or *critical* consideration when someone is being evaluated for advancement."

◆ Studies consistently find "that poor writing is a problem in the workplace," that new employees "tend to have a higher estimation of their own writing abilities than do their managers," and that "new college graduates are generally perceived as writing poorly." Eighty percent (80%) of the managers surveyed at 402 firms nationwide said that most of their employees need to improve their writing skills.

◆ According to *The Wall Street Journal*, a survey of 480 companies found that employers ranked communication abilities first among the desirable personal qualities of future employees.

◆ A survey of 1,000 human resource managers identified oral communication skills as crucial both in obtaining employment and in job performance.

2.2 ▌ Close Reading

Nervous in new shoes, I face a roomful of veterinary school interviewers who leaf through my transcript a little bemusedly, inquiring why my pre-veterinary required courses are so heavily interlarded with English classes. I understand their curiosity. Close reading of and analytical writing on essays and novels and even—ack—poetry? What could any of these academic exercises, they wonder, possibly have to do with the practice of veterinary medicine? A lot, I answer, with the first glow of confidence I have felt since entering this room. Both English and medicine require the same kinds of thinking—the ability to compare and connect disparate sources of information and to deduce a coherent and logical conclusion. In an English class, the material you are thinking about may be recurring images in a novel, or the application of a critical theory to a text, or the conflicting arguments of two articles you plan to use as source material for a research paper. In veterinary medicine, the sources may be physical examination findings, medical history, laboratory results, and symptoms. But in both cases, the process is the same: to see subtle or hidden connections and contradictions,

 to recognize and discard spurious or misleading information, to reconcile a collection of facts and impressions into a rational hypothesis, whether the hypothesis derived interprets a poem or diagnoses a sick animal.

And then the room relaxes into nods and smiles. At that moment, I know: I really can do this job and they are going to let me.

—Dr. Penny Livesay, BS, MA, DVM

In her comment on page 20, veterinarian Dr. Penny Livesay writes that close reading is the same process whether it's being used to analyze literature or diagnose a sick animal. No doubt any scientist would say something similar — to take data and discover its meanings, researchers must look carefully at detail, discern more than might be obvious at a glance, and relate the discovered information to a larger picture or puzzle. What else are they doing looking through microscopes but reading detail closely?

So why are you being asked to develop the skill of close reading in an English class? The answer may be simply that the texts you're examining, frequently fiction or other works of verbal or visual art, are probably more fun to read closely than stacks of printouts on the electrical conductance of concrete. You can learn the art of close reading and further the pleasure of a good read. And if the reading isn't to your liking, you can still develop your analytical skills without spending months placing probes into bridge decks. Your time may come to do that kind of vital research, but you won't be ready for it if you haven't learned to read closely.

Another reason for learning close reading by looking into written (or visual) works of art is that these works call on you to engage imaginatively with the human experience as explored by writers and artists. This kind of deep reading has been revered for millennia as a way of expanding our perceptions of the world — one of the essential acts of education. Close reading is an art in itself, one well worth practicing for your own intellectual growth.

So what is close reading?

First, close reading means reading several times. You can't do close reading on a first pass any more than a researcher can eyeball a bridge and know whether unseen cracks have allowed water to degrade the underlying rebar. The researcher has to come back to the bridge with instruments, perhaps many times under many conditions. In the same way, you have to come back to a text several times, with differing experiences to serve as diagnostic tools. One of the most basic aspects of close reading is re-reading.

Next, close reading is the process of discovering how much more you know about the text than you first thought. Close readers aren't looking for obscure symbols or codes that the author has deviously hidden in the text just to give teachers something to hold over students. Close readers are looking for ways that the text means things to them, for information carried not only in individual words (though that's a good beginning) but also in the structures of sentences, the patterns of associated words, or of repetition. The meanings that you can discover by close reading are not all the author's — they are partly yours.

2

Let's try it out on a short sample.

> The girl stepped along the dusty road, thumbs jammed under her faded suspenders, fingers drumming from time to time along with the tune she whistled.

OK. What kind of tune is she whistling? Slow? Fast? Happy? Melancholy? You do know. You have it in your imagination already. Write it down before you read further.

Most readers of this passage say the tune is "something cheerful," "jaunty," "peppy." No reader has ever said the tune was sad, melancholy, heavy, or solemn — and the experiment has been tried in many writing classes. Everyone thinks that it's a happy tune. You probably did too, though if you didn't, then you are in a position to do a most interesting alternative reading of the text.

For this discussion, let's assume that you did imagine an upbeat tune. So what made you imagine the tune to be happy, or at least energetic? Look closely.

"The girl": The word *the* suggests that we readers are supposed to know this girl. Even though we don't, we've been hooked into the fiction. *The* means "not just anyone, but this one that the writer/speaker and reader/hearer both know about." So already, the writer's choice of *the* has pulled us into the created world and generated a sense of familiarity. That doesn't tell us what she's whistling, but it does put us at ease.

"stepped along": What does this verb bring to mind? Something quite different from "walked," "trudged," "limped," "dragged," or "moped." To most readers, "stepped," to describe a continuous ambulation "along" a distance, brings up pictures of something slightly snappy. The words are not "stepped cautiously," or "stepped feebly." Rather, the girl "stepped along," reminding us of "step along smartly now!" You probably read that line in at least one children's story. A smart or snappy stepping does suggest that her music might be snappy as well.

"thumbs jammed under her faded suspenders": Even today, a girl wearing suspenders is a little unusual. Do we picture her as something of a tomboy? A fashion rebel? Further, she's not marching along like a soldier or striding like a serious hiker with a staff. She's taking it easy, resting her arms by supporting her hands in her suspenders. A tomboy taking it easy is not likely to be whistling a dirge.

"fingers drumming from time to time along with the tune she whistled": Occasionally, the music just can't be contained by her lips — it escapes and makes her fingers dance too. There's energy in it. She's enjoying it. It's got a fast enough rhythm to make finger-drumming fun, not likely with a funeral march.

Sentence structure: To examine what the structure of the sentence does for the mood of the tune, it will be helpful to think about the effects of another possible structure.

> The girl stepped along the dusty road. Her thumbs were jammed under her faded suspenders. Her fingers drummed from time to time along with the tune she whistled.

2

Most readers find that these short, simple, blunt sentences change the mood dramatically. The verbs are emphasized — *stepped, jammed, drummed.* The action seems more forceful, more deliberate, more serious, partly because the subject-verb structure is repeated and repeated. We readers are used to having the important part of a sentence spotlighted by the subject-verb structure, whether we know that's what it's called or not. So to have a string of three such structures, with full stops between, gives us a sense of three aggressive lunges of words.

Compare the effect of the original sentence — the phrases describing the thumbs' and fingers' actions trail along from the main action of stepping. They are attached, floating, flowing. This sentence rhythm produces a very different mood for most readers: relaxed, lighthearted. Though you hadn't consciously noticed this structural detail, it probably contributed to your initial, unexamined impression that the tune was a light or happy one.

OK — you knew what kind of tune to project in your mind, even after a first reading. Now, after close reading, you know how you knew. There are no secrets here, nothing hidden that only the teacher's master key can decipher. You just hadn't thought of these things — perhaps you haven't had much training or experience in close reading. That's what this exercise is meant to change.

■ *Practice*

You don't need much more instruction to get started. You've seen the process: pick a detail and play with what it tells you. Try your own close reading moves on the opening passage below from *The Mapmaker,* a novel by Virginia Tech faculty member Robin Mallory Allnutt.

The process suggested here can be applied to any text. Even if some of the language belongs to scholars, remember that you already know the answers — by the time you have read the passage even once, for example, you have already responded emotionally to the tone, and your mind has conjured images based on the text. You know the answers as surely as you knew what kind of tune the girl was whistling in our first example.

Step 1. Read the excerpt through one time, just to get a sense of the whole.

Step 2. Read it again slowly, letting the rest of the steps below guide you to specific textual observations.

Step 3. Pick out for particular consideration whatever words, phrases, lines, or passages are still troublesome. Be sure you understand the literal meaning of the words and can follow the structures of the sentences. In a dictionary or encyclopedia, look up names of places or persons, foreign words, references to mythology or special areas of learning.

Step 4. Try to paraphrase the passage as a whole, or perhaps just any part you find puzzling.

Step 5. Read the passage aloud. Often the need to construct a spoken melody for a sentence will help you comprehend it.

Step 6. Use some of the following questions to direct your attention to details. *NOTE:* These questions are provided to assist you in close reading of many texts. Not all of the questions apply to *The Mapmaker,* or indeed to any one text. They are here to show you just a few of the many analytical lenses that can help you focus on detail. For this practice, select questions that either work well with Allnutt's excerpt or those that spark your analytical imagination.

A. Who is the speaker? What kind of person is he or she? How do you know?

B. To whom is he or she speaking? What kind of person might the narrator be imagining as a listener or reader? What details give you clues?

C. What is the occasion? How can you tell?

D. What is the setting in time (time of day, season, century, etc.)? How do you know?

E. What is the setting in place (indoors or out, city or country, nation)? How do you know?

F. What do you find to be the central purpose of the passage?

G. State the central purpose in a sentence of your own.

H. Outline the passage to reveal its structure and development.

I. Discuss the tone—the emotional coloring. How is it achieved?

J. Discuss the diction—the words—of the passage. Point out words that strike you as significant and explain how they create meaning in the passage.

K. Discuss images you find in the passage—what strong visual and other sensual elements stay with you?

L. Do you find metaphor, simile, personification? Paradox, overstatement, understatement, irony? How do they color, affect, or create meaning?

M. Point out any allusions to familiar history, myth, scripture, or other literature. How do they affect your perception of the passage?

N. Point out instances of sound patterns. How do they affect you as a reader?

Step 7. Review your notes and form a question based on what you've observed. If you don't want to pursue any of the questions that occur to you, feel free to go forward with one of the following:

◆ Why might the narrator have to "dig" to find his grandfather?

◆ What might be buried under all this past?

◆ What role does "flight" have in this passage? What role might it have in the narrative to come?

Step 8. Write an exploratory paragraph using the details you have observed to answer your question.

---

from *The Mapmaker*

by Robin Mallory Allnutt

I was always digging as a boy. I had no idea then where it would lead. I started in the long slim back garden of our house on London Road with one of those cheap plastic trowels children use to build sandcastles and root through rock pools for washed up treasures. I probably used that same piece of rubbery blue plastic to uncover my first fossils along the sand and pebbly shores of Dorset, my first skull in the dust and dirt of an old playground. In my hunt, I soon graduated to child-size spades, then iron shovels with age-smooth wooden shafts, then steel blades, and back again to the soft tools of childhood I first used to dig up the past.

With my father and grandfather, though, I used a map.

The map was of my grandfather's making. "Richard," everyone called him, even me in those last years when he liked to hear his own name, my father's, and asked me to use them both. Richard was born at the turn of the century; "Before flight," Henry, my father, used to say. Henry liked to mark his own history with certain events, usually something to do with aeroplanes or rockets. I was born in 1969, "Just after the first lunar landing." Richard was born in 1903 before the Wright Brother's first flight that December. Though Henry never said it, he was born in Tanganyika just months before an English District Commissioner was speared in the middle of a cattle auction outside Arusha. On his map, Richard named that place Murder.

Richard had used pencil for all the names but that one, as though the other words might change at any moment, but that one was indelible. Some parts went unnamed. Where one would normally put names to features such as rivers or mountains or populated areas, Richard just left slim blank spaces, eventually filling each with his own additions. He spent much time renaming the world around him. Where one would logically expect to see Laetoli noted, there was the name Charlie. Shinyanga was named Henry for my father who was born there. The town of Henry was just South of Mare Incognita, or Lake Victoria. West of this Unknown Sea and slightly North of Lake Tanganyika (Mare Nostrum) were three tiny dots clustered into a pyramid in a part of the map that is now Southeast Burundi. Caput Nili was all the map read by the dots at the end of a slim curling blue line, a river, the source of the Nile. Further east, past Mare Incognita, Echo, Henry, and Charlie, almost tucked into a corner by The End, and The Aviatrix, was the place called Murder. Above it was a tiny cross.

Mysteries abound in this short passage, but the details hint at what may lie ahead in the novel. In this exercise in close reading, you become an explorer like the narrator, digging into a fictional world.

Readers seldom have an opportunity to learn what inspired an author. But the author of *The Mapmaker* has written the following commentary for readers of this textbook. In it, you may find details that support your reading. You may find completely new insights. You may find more questions. Enjoy.

Digging for the Truth

by Robin Mallory Allnutt

Every map tells the story of its maker. *The Mapmaker*, in truth, is as much a map of me, my own history, as it is of its fictional characters. The novel, set largely in the Tanganyika Territory of the late 1930s and early 1940s, is structured around a literal map made and given to the narrator, Hal, by his grandfather, Richard. The title of the first chapter, *Legend*, is a clue to its function (what does a map legend do?). Each of the subsequent chapters derives its name from a place on Richard's map. The patchwork quilt of nonlinear stories knits together three generations of one family and the secrets that haunt them.

The Mapmaker began as a series of homework assignments for a graduate creative writing workshop taught by my mentor, Susan Richards Shreve. Early on, the class had to write a "true" family story. I hadn't a clue where to start until my father told me about the death of his father's first wife, a woman I hadn't known about until that moment, and he linked it, without knowing, to something I had actually witnessed.

You have read the opening paragraphs of the novel. This is how my homework assignment began, and thus the first draft of the novel.

> In the early summer of 1989, a few months before he died, Richard removed himself from our family history. He spared nothing that bore his name, or likeness. All of it was put to the fire. He burned every word he could find, his diaries, his photographs, genealogical charts, even his early drawings of the source of the Nile. All that are left now are the map he gave me, and an old photograph of my Uncle Charlie that was taken three or four years after medical school when he was about my age.

The truth—my grandfather really died in 1987 in the fall of my freshman year at Virginia Tech. He burned everything sometime in June while I was visiting him in England for what he knew would be the last time. I had no idea what he was burning that day. It was seven years later when my father added the subtext to change my memory from an innocent backyard bonfire to something mysterious and upsetting to me. The journals Grandpa burned ranged from 1913 to 1987. He had written in them every day of his life from the age of six, when he had been put on a train by himself to go off to boarding school, to that day in June of 1987 when he erased himself.

The map, the photograph, and the uncle are fictions I invented to lead me to the real answers I sought. On my own map, my grandfather's secrets are unknowable. In fiction, I can invent everything, know everything. This is where the real and imagined worlds collide. A close reader might notice the uncle's name, Charlie or Char-lie, a lie from the charred remains of what really happened. In truth, I named the character Charlie after Charlie Allnutt of *The African Queen,* which is also set in colonial Tanganyika. It wasn't until I was editing (reading closely), much later, that I noticed the charred lie. Happy accidents are as welcome in fiction as they are in life.

So why did my grandfather burn all that family history? I don't know. *The Mapmaker* is my answer to that question. The truth is probably quite banal, but my fictional answer lies with Grandpa's first wife. Her name was Francis Armstrong, though I only found that name through considerable research. In *The Mapmaker,* I call her Lucy (she's "The Aviatrix" mentioned at the end of your excerpt), after the most famous hominid skeleton discovered in East Africa. I didn't have the name Francis Armstrong when I named the character. I was looking for a skeleton to flesh out so I named her after one. Like Charlie, the name resonates with recovered history. It also works subtly with the occupation of the narrator, Hal, a paleoanthropologist working on the restoration of the Laetoli Footprints (in the excerpt, this place is named "Charlie" on Richard's map).

The truth—when he was a colonial agricultural officer in the Tanganyika Territory, my grandfather met and married a woman called Francis Armstrong. She died of black water fever in the late 1930s. She was several months pregnant when she died. She refused medical treatment because she was a Christian

2

Scientist. My grandfather was away on official business and returned home to find his wife dead and buried, their first child still within her.

There was another wife and four more children, one of them, my father. The Tanganyika he remembers still holds the magic of childhood, though the place no longer exists. The borders have changed, and it is now the independent nation of Tanzania. Sometimes changes are literal, like the change of name and borders. More often, it is the quicksand of memory that shifts our perceptions, as mine did of my grandfather's "innocent" backyard bonfire. The England of my childhood no longer exists, if it ever did. The England of my grandfather's childhood was the largest and most powerful empire the world had ever seen to that point. Not anymore.

This theme of colonial decay runs throughout *The Mapmaker*. The strongest hint in the opening paragraphs is the phrase, "A part of the map that is now Southeast Burundi." It suggests, quite plainly, that it was once something else. The naming and renaming of places in the excerpt also reflects the colonial mindset and that of the mapmakers too. Maps themselves have been great tools for empires. Accurate maps went a long way toward giving the British navy an upper hand on its European rivals. The simple act of renaming can also be a powerful symbol of independence, of liberation, or even subversion in the case of African nicknames given to white "bwanas." Maps can also point to a more benevolent spirit of exploration, knowledge as an end in itself. *The Mapmaker* holds all of these ideas to be true, and they are there, implicit and explicit, in those first paragraphs along with the murder of an English District Commissioner.

"On his map, Richard named that place Murder."

"Richard had used pencil for all the names but that one, as though the other words might change at any moment, but that one was indelible."

Even in these first paragraphs, you know who is murdered right away and where and how, but not why, nor that he had it coming. The consequences of the "murder" are devastating. Richard is forced to make a terrible decision that results in the execution of his best friend, the dissolution of his marriage, and, ultimately, causes Lucy's death and the abandonment of their son (remember Charlie?). How did I get all that from a bonfire, a simple homework assignment? By reading closely, you can get a much better idea. Like my alter ego, "I was always digging as a boy." I still am.

2.3 ■ Thesis

What is a thesis?

A thesis is a statement of your essay's argument or point; it indicates in very specific terms the focus and direction of the essay. Your thesis is the arguable point that you want to "prove" in your essay. *For the purposes of most college writing assignments, the thesis is a single sentence located at the end of the first paragraph, previewing the logical divisions of the analysis or argument.* Your instructor may require this kind of thesis statement. Sometimes writers of highly complex arguments use several sentences (occasionally an entire paragraph) to articulate a paper's argument and purpose.

Must all essays have a thesis statement?

Narrative and descriptive essays frequently do not have explicit thesis statements, but all the essays you will write for English1105, English 1106, and English H1204, because they emphasize analysis, synthesis, and position, do require thesis statements.

What kinds of thesis statements will I be writing in Freshman Composition?

The kind of thesis you compose will vary with the assignment.

In general, the thesis statement for an *analysis* essay will show how you are breaking an idea into components *to reveal an underlying logic or examine relationships.* For example,

> Hamlet's baffling failure to act becomes understandable once we take into account his temperament, his religious beliefs, and his complex relationship with his mother.

The thesis statement for a *synthesis* essay will *orchestrate the voices or viewpoints of several writers in order to make a new claim.* For example,

> While the experts who spoke at a recent PBS symposium claim that proposed revisions to divorce laws would protect the interests of children, my own experience as a child of divorce convinces me that a further step is necessary: only when the courts require an attorney/advocate for the children, making them a party in the settlement with rights equal to those of their parents, will children truly be protected.

The thesis statement for a *position* essay *will assert an interpretive claim or argument, taking a stand that the essay will then support with compelling evidence.* For example,

> Shakespeare's Cleopatra is frequently dismissed as manipulative, hurtful, and scheming; a close reading of her role in *Antony and Cleopatra*, however, reveals a more complex and sympathetic figure characterized by vulnerability, courage, and a deep capacity for love.

What is a "working thesis" and how do I begin composing one?

Most writers need a tentative, or working thesis, in order to focus their thoughts. But if you are thinking carefully about your material, you will arrive at new and more complicated insights as you write. The resulting draft may not, then, finally support the original thesis. Good writers leave themselves open to new directions and insights, recognizing that the thesis should evolve, becoming more precise, complex, and original with each draft.

To begin, though, you will need that working thesis to get you going. Where does it come from? Writers generate a working thesis in a variety of ways. Perhaps one of these ways will work for you:

♦ Take notes on your assigned texts using the questions for close reading on pages 24–25. Based on these notes, freewrite for five minutes. Circle the best ideas and try to shape them into a claim or argument.

♦ Go through a four-step process of
   1. stating a general topic (for example, mining techniques)
   2. limiting the topic (strip mining techniques in Appalachia)
   3. asking questions about the limited topic (Why is it profitable? What are its effects on the ecosystem?)
   4. answering one of these questions in the form of a working thesis (Unregulated strip mining in Appalachia has had a devastating effect on the local ecosystem, giving rise to flooding, soil depletion, and environmental degradation.)

How do I revise my working thesis to make it stronger and more compelling?

Test your working thesis against the questions below and revise accordingly.

1. *Will readers be able to locate and identify the thesis?* Ask a friend to underline the thesis of your paper. If the task is difficult, you may need to move the thesis to a more predictable position (usually the last sentence in the first

paragraph). Or you may need to strengthen the claim, making sure that it is a claim rather than a mere assertion.

2. *Does the thesis go beyond a statement of fact, an observation, or a plot summary to assert a claim or make an argument?*

> **Factual statement/plot summary:** In "Aunt Jennifer's Tigers" the poet Adrienne Rich describes how her aunt used to weave a colorful tapestry with a jungle theme.

> **Argument:** In Adrienne Rich's "Aunt Jennifer's Tiger," stanza form and imagery build a feminist argument based on the gradually accumulating contrast between the vibrant scene depicted in the tapestry Aunt Jennifer weaves and the domesticated, subservient life she herself has led.

3. *Is the thesis limited and focused enough to be fully supported within the scope of the assignment?*

> **Too broad:** Americans must do everything possible to solve the energy crisis.

> **Limited:** Mounting evidence points to the feasibility of hydrogen-powered cars as one answer to our dwindling reserves of fossil fuels.

4. *Is the thesis unified, or does it loosely connect ideas that should really be developed in separate essays?*

> **Split focus:** In *The Poisonwood Bible,* Barbara Kingsolver critiques American consumer culture, and the book also deals with the theme of imperialism.

> **Unified focus:** In *The Poisonwood Bible*, Barbara Kingsolver juxtaposes characters, scenes, and cultures to expose the rampant materialism of American consumer culture.

5. *Does the thesis statement use clear, specific word choices within a readable, coherent sentence?* (Watch especially for pronouns without antecedents like "this" or "it" and specialized terminology that may need defining.)

> **Vague/confusing:** Asperger's Syndrome has been misunderstood because scientists don't understand the origins of this.

> **Clear:** Although the theory has won wide popular acceptance, a careful review of the evidence suggests that childhood vaccination is not the cause of Asperger's syndrome, a neurological dysfunction related to autism.

2

2

6. *Does the thesis provide appropriate guidance to the reader by suggesting the emphasis, method, or organization of your paper?*

> **No guidance:** Standardized testing has proven controversial in recent years.

> **Guidance:** The "No Child Left Behind" legislation should be repealed because it is rigid, it narrows the teaching/learning process, and it is an underfunded initiative.

7. *Is the thesis thought-provoking and original, or will it be obvious to readers, provoking a "so what" reaction?*

> **So what?:** In Charles Frazier's novel, *Cold Mountain,* the Civil War causes the main characters a lot of problems.

> **Original/thought-provoking:** [In Charles Frazier's novel, *Cold Mountain,*] those who are successful in the daily struggle for survival follow the Buddhist philosophy of viewing the world as an intricate web of relationships and connections tying together all living things.

Note: This thesis is from Sam Karty's prizewinning essay for *Composition: Writing, Revising, and Speaking, 2004–2005.*

Writer's Tools and Techniques

3.1 ▮ Summaries, Paraphrases, and Quotations

Summaries, paraphrases, and quotations are all ways of putting the work of other writers to work for you. **Whether you summarize, paraphrase, or quote another's work, you must clearly indicate the beginning and end of every borrowed passage.**

A summary is a *condensed version* of another writer's text. A good summary presents the writer's main ideas but eliminates all or most of the supporting details. It reduces a chapter to a paragraph or a paragraph to a single sentence.

A paraphrase is a *restatement* of another writer's text. A good paraphrase presents the writer's arguments, findings, and ideas in a passage approximately the same length as the original.

A quotation is an exact, word-for-word *replication* of the author's text.

▮ Using Summaries in First-Year Composition and Beyond

Summarizing is a skill you will use throughout your life — in your academic career, in your professional career, even in your everyday conversations with friends and co-workers. Certainly it is a skill you will be called on to use often in the First-Year Composition sequence.

In English 1105   In the Analysis and Synthesis papers, you will be asked to summarize the arguments of several writers and then analyze the differences in their views.

In the Position paper, you will almost certainly use summaries to provide evidence that supports your view, as well as to present arguments that oppose your view (which you will then, of course, try to counter or accommodate).

In English 1106/H1204   In research-based writing like the Contextualized Analysis and Research Papers, you will use summaries to give readers an overview of other writers' perspectives, thus bringing other voices into the conversation. You will also use your summarizing skills in compiling annotated bibliographies.

Beyond First-Year Composition   In most advanced studies and professions, you will continue to write summaries. At the senior, graduate, and professional levels, papers involving research usually include a literature review, in which you summarize the work of previous researchers who have contributed to the subject area. Publications in many fields will require you to provide an abstract of your paper, a condensed version that gives readers an idea of the whole in 100–200 words. Business and professional readers expect to see a lengthy report begin with an executive summary. Summary writing is a valuable skill that you can use in the future.

Summaries should be...

♦ **... short.** Summaries must be brief. Whether you set off a section of your essay devoted to a summary of one source or weave a few sentences of summary into your discussion, give readers just enough that they can follow your argument; don't try to re-create the entire original reading experience. Select main points, only occasionally including significant bits of supporting data for later reference.

♦ **... accurate.** Summaries must be absolutely accurate, presenting the original material without distortion, slant, editorializing, or evaluation; after you have summarized accurately, you can address areas of disagreement, merit, or fault.

♦ **... complete.** Though you must leave out most of the original, what you do present should be complete and coherent enough that readers will understand it without having read the original. The summary should be able to stand alone and make sense.

Incorporating Summaries into Papers

Your summary should include the following five essential elements:

1. an *introductory phrase* to indicate where the other writer's ideas begin
2. the *summary* itself
3. a *parenthetical notation of the page number(s)* where the material can be found in the original source
4. a *follow-up interpretive comment after the parenthetical citation* to integrate the summary smoothly into *your* essay
5. a *correctly formatted entry for the source material in a Works Cited page* at the end of your paper

■ *Using Paraphrases in First-Year Composition and Beyond*

Many college assignments will require paraphrasing. Some may simply ask you to study the work of several authors and then paraphrase what they have written. The more complex assignments will require that you integrate paraphrases into a larger project.

> *Writing well and speaking effectively*
> *are skills that need to be continuously*
> *developed and refined. Meaningful*
> *communication is essential for*
> *success in graduate work and all*
> *professional careers.*
>
> —Karen P. DePauw
> Vice Provost for
> Graduate Studies and
> Dean of the Graduate School

3

In English 1105   In the Synthesis and Position papers, paraphrases can help you develop your position. An author's argument may work to support and further your claims, so paraphrasing that author can be a surefire way of strengthening your position. While you may primarily want to paraphrase authors and articles that support your argument, keep in mind that after paraphrasing an opposing viewpoint, you can more effectively deal with the opposition.

In English 1106/H1204   In the Contextualized Analysis and Research Papers, you will also rely on the work of others to introduce, foreground, contextualize, and support your own ideas. Here too you will most likely be paraphrasing authorities who both support and oppose your position. In some cases, your paraphrase will have to "translate" technical jargon into language your audience can more easily understand. Like summaries, paraphrases allow you to put someone else's ideas to work for you. While you should always try to be fair and accurate in paraphrasing, remember that a paraphrase is a tool; you should paraphrase only what is necessary for *your* essay.

Paraphrases should be...

- ◆ **. . . thorough.** A paraphrase should be almost the same length as the original, presenting the same ideas and details in the same order, using your own words, and acknowledging and citing the source.

- ◆ **. . . accurate.** Paraphrases, like summaries, must be absolutely accurate, presenting the original material without distortion, slant, editorializing, or evaluation; after you have paraphrased accurately, you can address areas of disagreement, merit, or fault. Since you will be using words that are different from the author's, be careful to choose close synonyms, paying attention to connotation and context so as to represent the author's meaning as closely as possible.

Documenting Paraphrases

Your paraphrase should include the same five essential elements as the summary:

1. an *introductory phrase* to indicate where the other writer's ideas begin

2. the *paraphrase* itself

3. a *parenthetical notation of the page number(s)* where the material can be found in the original source

4. a *follow-up interpretive comment after the parenthetical citation* to integrate the paraphrase smoothly into *your* essay

5. a *correctly formatted entry for the source material in a Works Cited page* at the end of your paper

■ *Summary and Paraphrase: A Case in Point*

An example will help to clarify these summarizing and paraphrasing guidelines. Here is an article written by magazine writer and composition instructor Ed Weathers on the healthful benefits of burping, yawning, spitting, and sneezing. Read the article and try your hand at summarizing and paraphrasing it, using the guidelines printed above. Afterward, you can compare your attempts with Ed's, printed below.

NOTHING TO SNEEZE AT

**Why Mom's Rules Are
Bad for Your Health**

by Ed Weathers

Originally Published in
Memphis magazine (April 1989: 128)

DON'T LET YOUR MOTHER READ THIS. Send her out of the room.

She gone? Good.

I have a theory. It's a simple theory, really, and I'm not the first to think of it, but moms don't like it. The theory is this: *Good manners are bad for your health.* This is especially true of the good manners your mom insisted on when you were a kid—you know, the ones having to do with four-letter words like "yawn" and "spit" and "burp," plus others that I can't mention here even while Mom's out of the room. "Sneeze" has more than four letters, but it belongs here too.

Almost all the rules Mom imposed back then are bad for your health. When she told you not to yawn or burp in public, she was flying in the face of millions of years of carefully calibrated human evolution. We were designed to burp and yawn. When I repress a burp or squelch a yawn, I am defying Mother Nature in the name of Mother Weathers.

The fact is, our bodies are anachronisms. They are outdoor organisms in what has become an indoor world. They were designed to live in forests and on the plains, not in offices and on trains. They were designed to hunt and graze, not write memos and choose between forks. It took eons for nature to create the sneeze, which still performs an important health function. Okay, so today we live in conference rooms and restaurants, and sneezing there isn't as pleasant as sneezing outdoors. Nevertheless, it's still good for us.

I therefore recommend that we ignore our mothers and accept reality. I recommend that we legalize the public burp, yawn, and spit, and encourage the uncovered sneeze.

There. I've said it, and I'm not ashamed.

Let's begin with the burp. We burp because we swallow air when we eat. Everybody does it. Doctors call burping "eructation." Right after we burp, we automatically swallow a little more air, and pretty soon we have to burp again. It's as regular as breathing. If we didn't burp, our stomachs might explode. (In fact, there are cases on record of people who have gases in their stomach which have been known to literally explode, but that's something different.)

In many Near Eastern countries, of course, it is considered *de rigueur* for dinner guests to belch loudly after a meal, to express their satisfaction. Until the 17th century, the same was true in Europe. Then came fussy mothers. The prophet Muhammad preached that a belch, followed by the expression "Praise Allah," would help "avert seventy diseases, of which the least is leprosy." Wouldn't surprise me if he was right. Bring back the burp.

Likewise, the uncovered sneeze. Sneezing, along with coughing, is simply a way of preventing bad stuff like dust and bacteria from getting into the lungs. Thanks to sneezing, which doctors call "sternutation," lung tissue is almost completely free of microorganisms. Without sneezing, our nice warm, damp lungs would be a teeming hell of bacteria, and we'd be sick a lot. When you sneeze, you can rocket a germ up to twenty feet away. When you cover up a sneeze with your hand or handkerchief, you're missing the whole point, which is to get the bad stuff as far away as possible. Germs are much more likely to thrive on your wet, sweaty hand than on the ground, where they'll dry up and die.

3

3

When we sneeze, we go unconscious for a split second. Also, it is impossible to keep your eyes open when you sneeze. This is Mother Nature's way of keeping germs out of the eyes, which, modern doctors tell us, may be the conduits of cold germs. When we sneeze into our hands (as our mothers tell us to do) and then wipe our eyes or pick up the phone, we're probably giving somebody a cold.

Like burping, sneezing also has a distinguished history. Aristotle lumped yawning, sneezing, and belching together as "ejective" acts, but he considered sneezing more "sanctified" because it came from the head, not the belly. Folklore saw sneezing as a sign of life. A sick man who sneezed was thought to have a good chance to recover. In the Bible (2 Kings 4:35), the first sign that Elisha has brought a dead child back to life is when the child sneezes seven times. Some psychologists believe that a person who is able to let loose with a good sneeze is more likely to experience strong orgasms.

The next time you have to sneeze, ignore your mother, keep your hands down, and let fly. As a courtesy, make sure you're not aimed at anybody. Run outside first, if you have time.

As for spitting (let's keep this brief), it works about the same. When you've got germs, your mucous membranes increase the secretions to wash them away. You're better off expectorating the result than . . . well, any of the alternatives.

Spitting is seen world-wide as a way to bring good luck. Hence, fishermen spit on their hooks, and fighters spit on their hands. In some places, shopkeepers spit on the first money they get each day, for good luck; in other places, people spit on newborn babies as a blessing. Some experts say blowing a kiss is a variation of spitting for good luck. Spitting is good for you, Mom notwithstanding. Bring back the spittoon.

Let us end with the mild-mannered yawn. Your mother told you it is improper to yawn in public. She was wrong. A yawn is good for you. Experts have never really understood the yawn, but the latest medical theory has it that a yawn helps the lungs by forcing open the little air sacs (alveoli) that bring oxygen to the blood. Tibetans believe that a yawn, like sexual intercourse and dying, produces a higher state of consciousness. If somebody yawns in the middle of your next speech, consider that.

It's obvious that the world changes faster than evolution can keep up with; it will be another million years, for example, before a baby is born who is adapted to the electric light. Our bodies are still the same outdoor bodies that were designed to sneeze and spit in the wide open spaces. The world is now an indoor world of little ladies who tell us not to spit and sneeze in their kitchens. Their rules are not good for us.

But don't tell Mom I said that.

Here's how Ed himself would *summarize* his whole essay.

—*Note that because this summary is not part of a larger essay but simply an example of summarizing, Ed has included only the first two of the five essential elements of a summary: (1) the introductory phrase and (2) the summary itself. Not included are (3) the parenthetical notation of the page number(s), (4) the follow-up interpretive comment, and (5) the correctly formatted entry for the source material in a Works Cited page.*

> In his humorous essay "Nothing to Sneeze At," Ed Weathers lays out his theory that "good manners are bad for your health." Specifically, Weathers focuses on manners having to do with burping, sneezing, spitting, and yawning. Weathers' thesis is that stifling these acts in the name of good manners runs counter to human evolution and that we would be better off if we let ourselves burp, sneeze, spit, and yawn without constraint. He notes, for example, that evolution has designed burping as a way to vent stomach gases, sneezing and spitting as a way to get far from germs, and yawning as a way to increase our oxygen intake. He says modern manners—especially modern American manners—undercut these useful evolutionary purposes. Thus, for example, to cover up a sneeze (he says) keeps germs close when evolution demands that they be dispatched to a distance. Along the way, Weathers points out that in many other cultures, the acts of unconstrained burping, sneezing, spitting, and yawning are seen as valuable, even spiritual acts. His conclusion is that the rules of etiquette our modern mothers teach us are both provincial and bad for the health of our prehistorically evolved bodies.

Here's how Ed himself would *paraphrase* just the sneezing section of his essay.

—*Note that because this paraphrase is not part of a larger essay but simply an example of paraphrasing, Ed has included only the first two of the five essential elements of a paraphrase: (1) the introductory phrase and (2) the paraphrase itself. Not included are (3) the parenthetical notation of the page number(s), (4) the follow-up interpretive comment, and (5) the correctly formatted entry for the source material in a Works Cited page.*

> In the "sneezing" section of his essay "Nothing to Sneeze At," Ed Weathers points out that sneezing, or "sternutation," as doctors call it, is medically beneficial. He notes that sneezing expels dust and germs from our lungs and that a good sneeze can send bad microorganisms up to 20 feet away. He thus concludes that covering up a sneeze makes no sense, because it keeps the germs too close to us. When we cover a sneeze with our hands, Weathers says, we are just giving germs a good place to grow. Weathers supports this position by noting that our eyes always close when we sneeze—nature's way, he claims, of keeping germs out of our eyes. Finally, Weathers cites a list of cultures in which the sneeze has been viewed positively: Aristotle, he says, called the sneeze "sanctified" and even the Bible saw the sneeze as a sign of life. In conclusion, Weathers advises that we don't cover our sneezes—that we just run outside and sneeze unfettered.

■ Using Quotations in First-Year Composition and Beyond

Choosing appropriate quotations is important because appropriate quotations provide support and emphasis for your points; quotations strengthen your writing because they lend credibility to you and your writing.

Because you will be using the words and ideas of other writers, it is essential that you give the original authors their due credit. Beginning with a lead-in attribution, enclosing an author's words in quotation marks, and documenting the source using correct MLA format will help your readers find the original quoted material if necessary.

Introducing Quotations

When you use quotations, there are several basic related ideas that you must keep in mind.

- Never just paste a quotation into your text without linking it to your own sentence.
- Always use a lead-in to introduce the source and the quotation.
- Try to vary your sentence structure to create fluid, lively prose.

While it is often tempting to just paste a quotation into your text, you should never do so. It both disconcerts the reader and weakens your argument, suggesting that the quoted material is just an afterthought. Furthermore it disrupts the fluidity of your prose because the reader has to stop and figure out why, all of a sudden, there is a quotation, and how that quotation is supposed to be considered in relation to your argument. Consider the following examples.

Quotation is pasted in:

> The return of Selwyn's memory is complicated by issues of trauma and the resurgence of repressed memories. "I've never been able to sell anything, except perhaps, at one point my soul"(21). In re-scripting his own identity Selwyn sets in motion a series of developments that further widen the gulf between his identity (or as we can see, what Selwyn refers to as his "soul") and the process of denying that identity in the face of his history's new realities.

Quote is effectively integrated with an introductory comment:

> The return of Selwyn's memory is complicated by issues of trauma and the resurgence of repressed memories. **At one point Selwyn remarks that he has** "never been able to sell anything, except perhaps, at one point my soul" (21). In re-scripting his own identity Selwyn sets in motion a series of developments that further widen the gulf between his identity (or as we can see, what Selwyn refers to as his "soul") and the process of denying that identity in the face of his history's new realities.

Many verbs can be used to introduce quotations; here are the most commonly used and effective choices (mind you, there are many, many ways to introduce quotes and many word choices that are not listed here):

acknowledges	critiques	examines	questions
argues	describes	explores	remarks
concludes	discovers	points out	stresses
contends	emphasizes	proposes	summarizes

Example (from Ed Weathers' summary above):

> In his humorous essay "Nothing to Sneeze At," Ed Weathers *lays out* his theory that "good manners are bad for your health."

In the example above, you can see that the quotation has been effectively integrated into the author's own sentence.

While the verbs suggested above serve a purpose in allowing you to properly introduce your quotations, stringing together quotations even with effective verbs can weaken your prose by producing a stop-start pattern of reading. Furthermore, this pattern can limit how effectively you are able to make your argument about a text. Consider the difference between the following examples.

> Literary critic Emma Letley describes *Dr. Jekyll and Mr. Hyde* as a "portrait of a double consciousness." She says that the novel is "both universal and character-istically Scottish." She notes that "Stevenson himself also led something of a double life in the strict, Calvinistic confines of nineteenth-century bourgeois Edinburgh" (x).

In the example above the writer does *correctly* use quoted material. However, the basic sentence structure is repeated in each use of the quoted material, resulting in a monotonous, halting rhythm.

In the following example the prose is engaging, the quoted material is fully integrated and does not dominate the author's language, and each sentence flows into the next seamlessly.

> Like most readers of the novel from Stevenson's day to our own, literary critic Emma Letley sees *Dr. Jekyll and Mr. Hyde* as a "portrait of a double consciousness." The novel's theme of self-division is clearly part of its universal appeal, according to Letley, but, she argues, it is a preoccupation that is also "characteristically Scottish." Knowing that "Stevenson himself . . . led something of a double life in

> the strict, Calvinistic confines of nineteenth-century bourgeois Edinburgh," helps readers account for the unusual moral stance of the novel (x). In a radical move, Stevenson asks readers for empathy and understanding—both for the ambitiously righteous man and for his anarchic alter ego.

The second example is more readable, and it also shows that the writer has taken charge of the ideas and is using them in the service of an original argument.

Integrating and Documenting Quotations, Summaries, and Paraphrases

Most, but not all, composition classes require the Modern Language Association (MLA) format for documenting sources, as detailed in the *Prentice Hall Reference Guide,* Section 58. (Other formats are also described in the *Guide.*) Be sure to check with your instructor about which system to use.

When you document your sources, you indicate exactly where your words and ideas stop, where another person's words and ideas begin and end, and where your words and ideas pick up again.

There are five essential pieces to properly integrating and citing your sources:

- ◆ **The introductory or signal phrase:** This phrase usually (but not always) identifies the author of the quoted material, and it is essential in integrating quoted material into your text.

- ◆ **The word(s), phrase(s), or sentence(s) that you want to quote:** The quoted material should include only the passages that are relevant to your point.

- ◆ **The parenthetical citation:** If you have not named the author in the introductory phrase, what goes in the parenthetical citation should be the first element in the Works Cited entry for that source (author name, article title, etc.) along with the page number where the material can be found.

- ◆ **A comment on the material you have quoted:** This comment is essential because you cannot assume that your reader will understand why you have included a quotation. Make your reasons explicit with an analysis or an interpretation that relates to your point.

- ◆ **An entry in the Works Cited list, as required by MLA or another documentation style:** The Works Cited entry helps your reader find your source material in the event that he or she wants to read more from the text you quoted.

Each of these five elements is crucial to an effective use of another's material.

Examples: Let's say that you want to quote the following sentence from W. G. Sebald's novel *The Emigrants:*

> I changed my first name Hersch into Henry, and my surname Seweryn to Selwyn.

You would then follow these five steps to use the material effectively:

1. Use an introductory phrase (also called a *signal phrase* or *lead-in*) to indicate where your work ends and another person's work begins.

   In Sebald's novel *The Emigrant*, Selwyn says that upon his initial successes in the school systems of England

2. Then incorporate the material you are borrowing from a source, whether it is a direct quotation from a text, a paraphrase, factual material, or a summary.

   In Sebald's novel *The Emigrant*, Selwyn says that upon his initial successes in the school systems of England, **"I changed my first name Hersch into Henry, and my surname Seweryn to Selwyn."**

3. Then add the parenthetical citation of the page number(s) where the material can be found in the original source, which indicates where the other person's words and ideas end and your words and ideas begin again. Note that in this example, only the page number is needed in the parenthetical citation because the author is identified in the introductory phrase.

   In Sebald's novel *The Emigrant*, Selwyn says that upon his initial successes in the school systems of England, "I changed my first name Hersch into Henry, and my surname Seweryn to Selwyn" **(20).**

4. Then follow the parenthetical citation with an analytical comment to weave the quotation into *your* paper.

   In Sebald's novel *The Emigrant*, Selwyn says that upon his initial successes in the school systems of England, "I changed my first name Hersch into Henry, and my surname Seweryn to Selwyn" (20). **In a characteristically oblique manner, Sebald positions subjectivity against material realities. While this change in his name seems innocent enough, it also shows the way in which Selwyn subsumes his own identity and ethnicity in an attempt to naturalize himself to England's conventions.**

3

5. Then you simply add a correctly formatted entry for the source of the other writer's material in a Works Cited page at the end of your paper. There is an extensive discussion of the Works Cited page in the *Prentice Hall Reference Guide,* Section 58c.

> Sebald, W. G. *The Emigrants.* Trans, Michael Hulse. New York: New Directions, 1996.

You can vary the basic sentence structures when you incorporate quoted material. We'll use this quotation from an article by Walter Cohen in the following examples.

> Venetian reality during Shakespeare's lifetime contradicted almost point for point its portrayal in the play.

Examples of integrated quotations:

> **One author notes that** "Venetian reality during Shakespeare's lifetime contradicted almost point for point its portrayal in the play" (Cohen 770).

> "Venetian reality during Shakespeare's lifetime contradicted almost point for point its portrayal in the play," **according to Cohen** (770).

> **Cohen argues that** "Venetian reality during Shakespeare's lifetime contradicted almost point for point its portrayal in the play" (770).

> "Venetian reality during Shakespeare's lifetime," **Cohen points out,** "contradicted almost point for point its portrayal in the play" (770).

> **In comparing and contrasting English and Italian economic practices at the time, Cohen finds that *The Merchant of Venice* is in no *real* way indicative of the actual economic practices of the nations themselves:** "Venetian reality during Shakespeare's lifetime contradicted almost point for point its portrayal in the play" (770).

Note that when the author is identified within the sentence, the author's name is omitted from the parenthetical citation.

Remember: Never just drop a quotation into your paper. Lead into it with a word or phrase that connects it with the previous phrase or sentence, and follow up the quotation with a comment that guides the reader back into your argument.

Short Quotations: Any quotation that is shorter than four typed lines should be placed inside quotation marks and carefully integrated into your sentence. The citation for your quotation should be placed between the ending quotation mark and the sentence's closing punctuation. Keep in mind, though, that when you do not identify the author in your lead-in, or if it is not contextually evident which source you are quoting from, you must include the author's name in the parenthetical citation along with the page number.

> Touring the estate, Selwyn comments that the tennis court "has fallen into disrepair, like [. . .] so much else around here" (Sebald 7). Instead of being a place of repose, the landscape totters on memory's fringes, growing out of the space of a time now irretrievably lost to the logical outcome of its own designs: set to master the world, human construction follows nature's course in wilting, rotting, and crumbling away.

Block Quotations: When quotations are longer than four typed lines, they should be indented ten spaces from the left margin, but the right margin is not changed. Note also that block quotations should be double-spaced along with the rest of your paper. When you use block quotations, do not use quotation marks, except for when you are quoting dialogue or if quotation marks are in the original text. Another important point is that in block quotations the parenthetical citation goes outside the punctuation mark at the conclusion of your quotation. Refer to the example below:

> In the early works before their marriage, both Plath and Hughes explore ideas of whether interdependence can co-exist with a person's expressions of independence. However, Hughes' concern with this mutuality, a central theme in his 1957 *Hawk in the Rain,* clearly derives directly from a 1952 journal entry by Plath written four years before their marriage:
>
> > What is it but destruction? Some mystic desire to beat to sensual annihilation—to snuff out one's identity on the identity of the other—a mingling and mangling of identities? A death of one? Or both? A devouring and subordination? No, no. A polarization rather—a balance of two integrities, changing, electrically, one with the other, yet with centers of coolness, like stars (And D.H. Lawrence did have something after all—) [. . .] But fusion is an undesirable impossibility—and quite non-durable. So there will be no illusion of that. (105)
>
> What this journal entry shows in Plath's typically violent expressions, and what *Hawk in the Rain* explores in less vitriolic language, is the impossibility of the independent mind integrating into interdependence with and upon another.

Note: We have single-spaced our published examples, but in all manuscripts, including academic papers, you should double-space throughout, *including any block quotations.*

Punctuating Quotations Correctly

Punctuating quotations is complicated because the material within the quotation marks must be reproduced exactly as it appears in the original, but the original does not always exactly suit your sentence. Detailed guidelines and examples for the process in the

Prentice-Hall Reference Guide sections **31** and **56d** cover most situations including quotations of both prose and poetry.

Removing Unnecessary Material from within a Quotation

If part of the quoted material is not necessary for your purpose, use three spaced *ellipsis dots* in *brackets* to replace material you remove. The brackets indicate that you have added the ellipsis dots, and the dots indicate that material has been removed.

If you leave out a whole sentence or more, end the sentence before the deletion with its original punctuation, then insert the bracketed ellipsis dots to show that material has been left out:

> Hill explains in her essay that "carefully reading the recipe is paramount to the success of cooking. [. . .] It is the careless chef whose recipes fail" (233).

If you leave out material from within a single sentence, simply insert the bracketed ellipsis dots in place of the deleted word or words.

> According to Johnson, "When traveling abroad [. . .] make sure to have all of your required documents with you" (32).

3.2   Understanding Plagiarism

To avoid plagiarizing—a serious academic and even legal offense—you will need to make certain that you know how and when to document sources. Documenting sources properly is an ethical responsibility; honesty requires that you acknowledge the ideas and language of others. It is also a courtesy to readers who may want to locate the original source in order to read and study further. Different disciplines use different formats, but three aspects of the documentation process are universal:

◆ The writer must indicate exactly where *every* piece of cited material begins and ends in the paper (using quotation marks to denote direct quotations and signal phrases to indicate other borrowings).

◆ The writer must provide some type of reference for every piece of cited material.

◆ The writer must provide a list of all sources used, arranged according to the conventions of the discipline.

The basic principles of documentation are covered in the *Prentice Hall Reference Guide* (section **58**). The specific documentation methods used should follow the format prescribed by the instructor or by a specific manual.

■ *Is Your Essay Plagiarized? A Trouble-Shooting Checklist*

Plagiarism, defined as representing another's work as your own, comes in many forms — from deliberate, word-for-word copying to the inadvertent omission of a source for a paraphrased idea. To make certain that you have avoided any form of plagiarism, study the passage below and the numbered examples showing inappropriate uses of source material. Check to make sure that you are not guilty of the italicized problems.

Refer to the passage below and the numbered examples before turning in your paper.

> ORIGINAL TEXT: "If the waking world has certain advantages of solidity and continuity, its social opportunities are terribly restricted. In it we meet, as a rule, only the neighbors, whereas the dream world offers the chance of intercourse, however fugitive, with our distant friends, our dead, and our gods. For normal men it is the sole experience in which they escape the offensive and incomprehensible bondage of time and space" (102).
>
> Dodds, E. R. *The Greeks and the Irrational*. Boston: Beacon, 1957.

1. *Plagiarism—Word-for-word continuous copying without quotation marks or mention of the author's name:*

> Dreams help us satisfy another important psychic need—our need to vary our social life. This need is regularly thwarted in our waking moments. *If the waking world has certain advantages of solidity and continuity, its social opportunities are terribly restricted. In it we meet, as a rule, only the neighbors, whereas the dream world offers us the chance of intercourse, however fugitive, with our distant friends.* We awaken from such encounters feeling refreshed, the dream having liberated us from the here and now.

2. *Plagiarism — Copying many words and phrases without quotation marks or mention of the author's name:*

> Dreams help us satisfy another psychic need—our need to vary our social life. In the *waking world* our *social opportunities*, for example, *are terribly restricted. As a rule,* we usually encounter *only the neighbors*. In the dream world, on the other hand, we have the chance of meeting *our distant friends*. For most of us it is the *sole experience in which* we *escape* the *bondage of time and space.*

3. *Plagiarism — Copying an occasional key word or phrase without quotation marks or mention of the author's name:*

> Dreams help us satisfy another psychic need—our need to vary our social life. During our waking hours our *social opportunities are terribly restricted.* We see only the people next door and our business associates. In contrast, whenever we dream, we can see *our distant friends.* Even though the encounter is brief, we awaken refreshed, having freed ourselves from the *bondage* of the here and now.

4. *Plagiarism — Paraphrasing the passage — expressing its meaning in your own words — without mention of the author's name:*

> Dreams help us satisfy another important psychic need—our need to vary our social life. When awake, we are creatures of this time and place. Those we meet are usually those we live near and work with. When dreaming, on the other hand, we can meet far-off friends. We awaken refreshed by our flight from the here and now.

5. *Plagiarism — Taking the author's idea without acknowledging the source:*

> Dreams help us to satisfy another important psychic need—the need for change. They liberate us from the here and now, taking us out of the world we normally live in.

6. *Plagiarism — Quoting, paraphrasing, or summarizing a source without explicitly indicating when you are doing so, even if you have elsewhere acknowledged this source.*

■ Understanding "Common Knowledge"

"Common knowledge" is a somewhat ambiguous concept. How can you know if an idea or a fact can be considered common knowledge, one that requires no documentation? Here are a few general guidelines:

1. Concepts and facts *widely known* outside the specific area of study are generally considered common knowledge. These include undisputed dates (e.g., the adoption of the Declaration of Independence on July 4, 1776), scientific principles (e.g., Newton's Laws of Motion), and commonly accepted ideas (e.g., Hamlet's role as a tragic hero). Such data require no specific reference. Students should be aware, however, that the addition of minor informational embellishments might require documentation (e.g., that the Declaration of Independence was unanimously adopted by the American colonies on July 4, 1776, despite the abstention of New York).

2. The fact that material appears in a dictionary, encyclopedia, handbook, or other reference work or textbook does not guarantee that it is common knowledge. Such books are written by experts, and most of the information they contain is not widely known.

3. There is no simple test to determine whether information is common knowledge. When in doubt, consult your instructor.

Given the seriousness of plagiarism, prudent writers cite a reference whenever they are uncertain.

3

3.3 ■ Developing Style

All good writers have their own voices by which we can recognize them — certain distinctive rhythms, word choices, sentence patterns, and the like. These features are sometimes lumped together under the general category of style. While no one voice or style is intrinsically better than another, if you wish to write well — that is, if you wish to write vivid, memorable, persuasive, elegant prose — the following advice can help you.

Be specific.

Whenever you use a generality, follow it with at least one specific example.

> GENERAL: In *Cold Mountain,* Ada learns for the first time to do many farm chores on her own.
>
> SPECIFIC: She learns, for example, to plant corn, milk cows, build fences, and even plow the fields.

> GENERAL: Faulkner suggests in *The Bear* that animals may demonstrate virtues normally considered to be limited to humans.
>
> SPECIFIC: The dog Lion goes after the bear with the single-minded persistence and self-possession of the best human hunter; the one-eyed mule stands fast with what seems to be human courage and intelligence in the face of the bear's scent; and Old Ben — The Bear himself — endures, thanks to his superhuman wit and nearly godlike wisdom, until he's killed by the human Boon, who, ironically, has none of the above virtues himself.

> GENERAL AND SPECIFIC IN THE SAME SENTENCE: In Bill McKibben's book *Enough,* it is clear that the author distrusts most new technologies, from robotics and artificial intelligence to genetic engineering and cryogenics—from chess-playing computers to mice that stay forever young.

Note that specific examples do two important things for your writing: First, they make it clearer, more vivid, and more memorable. Second, they serve as evidence that gives authority to your general ideas; they prove your point. Specific textual evidence is essential when you are making a point about any text.

Style tip: Many Virginia Tech faculty members have said that they find themselves immediately biased against a paper as soon as they read unspecific or inaccurate terms, especially the overused noun "society," the misused adjective "unique," and the inaccurate (in most instances) verb "states." You will do well to avoid these trigger terms—what they may trigger is the reader's expectation of weak thinking by means of unspecific language.

Be precise.

Choose words that convey the most information most accurately. Avoid vague or empty words.

> IMPRECISE: I should interact with my professor occasionally.
>
> PRECISE: I should meet with my professor in his office at least weekly.
>
> PRECISE: I should e-mail my professor daily.

> IMPRECISE: In *Catch-22*, Yossarian has an awesome personality.
>
> PRECISE: In *Catch-22*, Yossarian speaks truths that the army cannot allow to be spoken.

> IMPRECISE: In *Pride and Prejudice*, Elizabeth Bennett's intelligence is incredible.
>
> PRECISE: In *Pride and Prejudice*, Elizabeth Bennett sees through everyone's public persona except that of the man she comes to love.

> IMPRECISE: *To the Lighthouse shows* how domestic life relates to people's feelings about themselves.
>
> PRECISE: *To the Lighthouse* suggests that, to value herself, a woman must feel that she is raising her children and running her household well.

Most of the time, use action verbs in the active voice.

Generally, this means showing people doing things. Making the actors the subjects of your sentences will add muscle and energy to your writing. It will also make your prose more concise and help you avoid some common grammar errors. Be aware that forms of the

Your writing, perhaps more than any other single element, can distinguish you from others if you learn to write well. More importantly, it provides you with one of the most important tools you can carry into your professional and personal life. Writing well enables you to share your ideas and feelings in meaningful ways with your associates, friends, and family: it empowers you to make a difference in the lives of others through your thinking.

—Jerome A. Niles
Dean of the College of Liberal Arts and Human Sciences

verb "to be," especially in "it is" or "there is" phrases, slow sentences down and deflect the action. Passive constructions have a similar effect (see the *Prentice Hall Reference Guide to Grammar and Usage,* sections **14f** and **17d**).

> PASSIVE VOICE LEADING TO DANGLING MODIFIER: Going to the store, five traffic lights had to be driven through.
>
> ACTIVE: Going to the store, we drove through five traffic lights.

> "TO BE" VERB: The cause of Gatsby's death is his belief in his own dream.
>
> ACTIVE: Gatsby dies because he believes in his own dream.

> "TO BE" VERB, PASSIVE VOICE: There are twelve ways that the whale is described by Ishmael.
>
> ACTIVE: Ishmael describes the whale in twelve ways.

Note: There's nothing wrong with passive-voice verbs, but use them only when the situation calls for passive voice:

◆ *When you don't know who performed the action:*

> My house was broken into while I was on vacation.

♦ *When you want to emphasize the receiver of the action:*

> The gun bill was passed by the Senate.
>
> *This passive sentence emphasizes which bill passed.*

> The Senate passed the gun bill.
>
> *This active sentence emphasizes which body of Congress passed the bill.*

♦ *In some scientific writing:* Scientists and social scientists often use the passive voice when describing experiments and studies, to emphasize the experiment rather than the scientist and what is observed rather than the observer:

> The placebo test was conducted on 15 patients.
> The villagers' burial rites were observed over a period of 15 months.

Be concise.

Don't use many words where one word will do.

> WORDY: He was cognizant of the fact that Moby Dick was the cause of Ahab's lost leg.
>
> CONCISE: He knew that Moby Dick had bitten off Ahab's leg.

> WORDY: Due to the fact that Elizabeth had the belief that D'Arcy possessed little compassion, she had no expectations that he would provide help for her sister.
>
> CONCISE: Elizabeth believed that D'Arcy lacked compassion, so she didn't expect him to help her sister.

> WORDY: The big fat man sat on the soft, fluffy dog in the white snow.
>
> (Which words could you remove from this sentence without changing its meaning?)

Vary your sentences.

A long series of compound/complex sentences can be tedious. So can a long series of simple sentences. Thus you will want to vary your sentences — especially the length of your sentences. The following paragraph illustrates how you can vary sentence length, use balance and parallel structure, invert subject and verb, even employ sentence fragments to good effect.

Example:

> Ray Bradbury's *The Martian Chronicles* makes a strong statement against capital-
> ism. Though the story is set in the future, the Earthlings who arrive on Mars
> bring with them the values of post–World War II capitalist America: a love of
> banks and skyscrapers, mines and paved roads—all the trappings of a commer-
> cial society. These Earthlings immediately build hot dog stands and general
> stores. Why? So they can turn a quick buck. Or, preferably, a quick *million* bucks.
> In the process, the Earthling capitalists destroy the ancient Martian cities, whose
> buildings are as elegant as ivory chess pieces, and, with their broken whiskey
> bottles and cigarette butts and coffee grounds, they pollute the pristine rivers of
> the Martian landscape. What they don't understand, the Earthlings corrupt. What
> they can't corrupt, they destroy. Gone, before long, vanished from their own
> planet, are the Martians themselves. And left hanging in the sky, cracked by a
> nuclear war fought for government bonds and Wall Street stocks, is the ashen,
> bankrupt Earth.

3

Write assertively. Don't water down your writing with unnecessary qualifications.

Avoid unnecessary "not" constructions:

> WEAK: She was not often on time.
> STRONGER: She was usually late.

Avoid de-intensifiers like "somewhat" and "rather" when you can replace them with more assertive constructions:

> WEAK: He felt somewhat afraid of crossing the bridge.
> STRONGER: He trembled at the idea of crossing the bridge.

Avoid using verbs like "would," "might," and "may" if they will make your writing sound wishy-washy:

> WEAK: Twain might be saying that Huck has always been an orphan.
> STRONGER: Twain implies that Huck has always been an orphan.

Above all, be clear.

Ignore any of these rules to make your writing easier to understand.

3.4 ▊ Taming Technology: The Promise and Perils of Spell Checkers, Grammar Checkers, and E-mail

Learning to use technology effectively is one key to succeeding in first-year composition. Students who know the limits of their word-processing programs and who can communicate effectively with e-mail are ready to make technology work for them.

▊ *Spell Checkers: Useful for Final Drafts*

Spelling is obviously important. Misspellings not only create confusion, but they also suggest that the writer is incompetent, careless, or both, so writers need to be careful with spelling. However, worrying about spelling early in the writing process diverts attention from more important matters — like thesis, focus, organization, and development. And it makes no sense to worry about spelling in early drafts because the word(s) in question may not even appear in the final draft. We suggest that you use your spell checker only after you have finished revising your essay.

However, keep in mind that your spell checker can check only spelling; it cannot proofread your text. If you want the word "flying" but type "fling," the spell checker will not catch the error. Only human eyes can recognize "fling" as an error here. Likewise, spell checkers cannot detect "sound-alike" errors. If you want "except" but type "accept," the computer won't catch the error. Spell checkers cannot detect "spacing" errors in compound or hyphenated words. If you want "skyline" but type "sky line," the computer won't catch the error, and if you want "computer-aided" (as an adjective meaning "with the help of a computer") but type "computer aided," the computer won't catch the error either.

Spell checkers have only a few thousand words pre-programmed into their lexicons. Since every discipline has its own set of specialized terms, you will need to learn how to add these words to the lexicon. In Microsoft Word, when the spell checker flags one of these words, simply click the "Add to Dictionary" button to add the word.

■ *Grammar Checkers: Proceed with Caution*

The grammar checkers that come with word-processing programs would seem to free writers from the tedious task of proofreading for errors, but be warned that this technology is simply not very reliable. Because grammar checkers cannot read, they rely on crude comparisons between your sentences and a limited range of model sentences. In other words, grammar checkers classify your words as nouns, verbs, and modifiers, and then try to identify the relationship between these words. Once the program has converted your sentences into something it understands, it checks them against the models.

This process commonly results in two kinds of problems:

◆ Correct sentences that are simply longer than average or more complex are flagged as errors.

◆ Many common errors, like shifts in verb tense or pronoun errors, are often overlooked.

Used with attention, grammar checkers can provide useful information. They consistently identify passive voice, for example. *But unless you are willing to invest time in learning how the program works and how to customize it, and unless you use your handbook and your own careful proofreading to supplement and cross-check, you would be better off turning the grammar checker off.*

If you enjoy experimenting with software programs, here are some tips for using grammar checkers strategically:

◆ **Customize the kind of feedback you receive.** Most programs will highlight errors as you type or allow you to move through your work error by error when you choose to do a check. You can customize both of these types of feedback or simply turn them off.

◆ **Check errors with a grammar guide.** Just as you shouldn't run a spell checker without a dictionary on hand, you shouldn't run a grammar checker without a grammar guide on hand. Grammar checkers aren't always correct, and if you don't understand the error or the correction, then you should consult a handbook.

◆ **Turn off consistently incorrect rules.** If the program is consistently incorrect about a particular rule, tell the grammar checker to ignore that rule. Microsoft Word, for instance, lets you "Ignore All" errors in a document while checking, and even allows you to turn rules off in Preferences.

◆ **Review the grammar checker's suggestions.** Not only will grammar checkers miss errors, they may also suggest corrections that are wrong or confusing for a human reader. Review any suggestions for errors, and remember to consider how a corrected sentence will work with the text around it.

■ *E-mail: Presenting Yourself as a Serious Student*

E-mail is an easy and effective way to communicate with your instructors, but e-mail within the university is somewhat different from e-mail in the outside world. We offer the following advice to help you write effective e-mail:

◆ Use your Virginia Tech e-mail account for Virginia Tech business. The VT information system for class rosters, e-mail lists, and the like assumes that you will use your VT account.

◆ Before writing to your instructor, ask yourself if e-mail is appropriate. Complex matters are usually better handled in face-to-face meetings with your instructor.

◆ Be patient. Don't assume that your message has been lost if you don't receive a speedy reply.

◆ You may create an alias for your e-mail account, but do so judiciously. (See http://answers.vt.edu and select "E-mail.") Changing your e-mail address to something more human sounding (from brwhite6@vt.edu to Bradley.White@vt.edu) makes sense. But don't use unprofessional e-mail addresses (like anarchist@vt.edu).

◆ Remember that e-mail is not private: a recipient might choose to send a note to others or print out your note to share.

◆ Before hitting "Send," be sure the "To:" line is correct. It can be very embarrassing when a personal message gets sent out to the class e-mail list.

◆ Pay attention to spelling, grammar, punctuation, and word usage. Your reader will form an opinion of you based upon the text you send.

◆ Use carefully worded, meaningful subject lines. Readers use them to gauge the importance of the message.

Words are our way of connecting with those around us, and the written word is our amplifier to connect with many people at once, notwithstanding the confines of time and geography.

—Lay Nam Chang
Dean of the College of Science

3

◆ Focus each e-mail message on a single topic. For multiple topics, use multiple messages, each with a distinctive subject line.

◆ Begin the message with a salutation, such as "Dear Professor Jones."

◆ Create clear and informative signature files. Include your e-mail address, phone number, and post office address. Resist the temptation to affix your favorite quotation to the end of your signature file. Recipients who see the same quotation in every single message may eventually feel annoyed, or worse.

◆ Do not use emoticons such as :-) ;-) :-(or instant-messaging-style abbreviations, such as IMHO (in my humble opinion), LOL (laughing out loud), or F2F (face to face) in formal e-mail to professors or employers.

◆ If you are responding to a previous message, include at least the specific part(s) to which you are responding, if not the whole previous message. The reader may need the reference and may not wish to sort through dozens or hundreds of messages to find earlier e-mail. If the correspondence continues, keep at least the relevant portions of the message chain intact to assist your reader.

◆ Be concise.

◆ Double-space between paragraphs.

◆ Use lists to keep messages short and direct.

E-mail to your instructor should NOT look like this . . .

> To: kvsmith@vt.edu
> From: brewmeister783@yahoo.com
> Subject:
> Cc:
> Bcc:
> Attachments:
>
> i wuz wondering if we did anything importnat in class yesterday. also, i
> didn't understand you're last message to the class. : - (didja see that UVa
> lost again!!!!!! LOL
>
> L8R

. . . but rather like this:

> To: kvsmith@vt.edu
> From: Tim.Perkins@vt.edu
> Subject: making an appointment?
> Cc:
> Bcc:
> Attachments:
>
> Dear Professor Smith,
> I wanted to talk with you about some of your comments on my Analysis paper,
> but I can't make your regular office hours. Would you be available to meet
> sometime next Wednesday?
>
> Tim Perkins
> ENGL 1106—Tuesday/Thursday, 9:30

3.5 ■ Receiving and Responding to Feedback

A paper that you get back from your instructor will most likely contain the following kinds of written feedback:

◆ *Editing marks* — may be formal or informal: used to point out errors in grammar, usage, punctuation, spelling, mechanics, or formatting.

◆ *Margin notes* — may be statements or questions: most often used to communicate the reader's response while in the process of reading the essay.

◆ *End comment* — may be written on your paper or distributed separately: used to give an overall impression of a paper's strengths and weaknesses; often reviews the general or repeated errors appearing throughout the paper.

◆ *Rubric*—a separate grid or check sheet: rubrics break down the characteristics for successful completion of the assignment. They show you at which points your paper is successful or unsuccessful.

◆ *Grade*—a number or a letter grade: tells you how well you met the instructor's expectations for the particular assignment.

How can you use your instructor's comments constructively—that is, to improve your writing? We suggest that you think of your interaction with your instructor as a semester-long conversation made up of a series of smaller conversations.

Your instructor began one of these smaller conversations with an assignment. You replied by writing your paper. Your instructor then responded with comments and/or a grade on your paper.

Now what? If you have a minor question about the comments, you can talk to your instructor about it before or after class. If you have more serious questions, you can schedule an appointment with your instructor to talk about the paper. If you do schedule an appointment, keep in mind that your instructor will assume that you have re-read your paper and have carefully read all the comments before the meeting.

You can also respond to your instructor's comments in writing. Some instructors will have procedures in place for this kind of response. They may ask you to keep a log of your grammar mistakes, for example, or to write a journal entry about the feedback you received on an essay.

Ideally, you will continue the conversation with your instructor by using the comments made on previous papers to improve your work in future papers.

3.6 ■ Seeking Additional Help: The Role of the Writing Center

The Writing Center can provide valuable one-on-one help with your writing. You can find detailed information about the Virginia Tech Writing Center at the following address: http://www.english.vt.edu/wc.

What Writing Center Tutors Can and Can't Do

Writing Center tutors can help you with almost any writing problem, large or small, but they can't do your work for you. Tutors can help students think through an assigned topic, help them develop a thesis statement, and help them organize an essay, but tutors may not write the thesis statement or organize the paper. Tutors can help students with rough drafts by pointing out grammar, punctuation, usage, and format errors (among others), but tutors may not correct those errors. Don't think of the Writing Center as a "fix-it" shop; think of it as a place where you can get personalized instruction that will help you become a better writer.

How to Contact the Writing Center

The Writing Center is located in *340 Shanks Hall;* the phone number is *231-5436*. You can call or stop by the Writing Center to make an appointment; walk-ins are welcome, but walk-ins can be seen only if an on-duty tutor is free. Hours vary each semester, but the Writing Center is usually open from 9:00 to 4:00, Monday through Friday. Some evening hours may also be available.

The busiest times for the Writing Center are midterm and the end of the semester. Call two or three days in advance at those times to schedule an appointment.

4

Analysis

4.1 ■ The Analysis Assignment

■ ENGL 1105—Analysis I

1st Essay in ENGL 1105: Essay #1 in the
Composition Sequence

Overall Goal: to learn the techniques of detailed critical analysis through examination of a single short text

General Assignment: Explore the relationship between a single text (a short set of poems, a short story, a short novel or drama, or a short work of nonfiction) and some aspect of the course theme.

■ ENGL 1106/H1204—Analysis II

1st Essay in ENGL 1106/H1204: Essay #4 in the
Composition Sequence

Overall Goal: to refine and extend analytical proficiency through examination of a single long text

General Assignment: Explore the relationship between a single text (an extensive set of poems, a full-length novel or drama, or a book-length work of nonfiction) and the larger issues of the course.

■ Skills/Criteria for Analysis I and II:

Each essay should demonstrate your ability to accomplish the following:

- develop and maintain a focused thesis that explains the relationship between the text and a core theme or issue in the course
- analyze a text in detail
- support that analysis with textual evidence
- relate that analysis to a theme/issue/idea outside the text
- support that relationship with concrete evidence (class notes, experience)
- organize the essay to develop the thesis effectively
- write according to the accepted academic standards for grammar, mechanics, punctuation, and spelling

4

Effective communication skills are required for anyone who wants to be successful in business. Business professionals are often called upon to be able to communicate effectively with large numbers of people in order to achieve the goals of the business. To be effective, a businessperson must have well-developed writing skills as well as a strong command of the language.

—Richard E. Sorensen
Dean of the Pamplin College of Business

4

4.2 ■ What Is Analysis and Why Is It Important?

When we analyze something, we break it down into its component parts so that we can discover how those parts work together to produce the whole. Analysis allows us to experience what physicist Richard Feynman calls "the pleasure of finding things out." If we can't analyze for ourselves, we can only learn by rote, which means we can only know what others want us to know. Analysis is thus not only *the* key element in real learning, it is ultimately a liberating behavior, allowing us to find out the "how" and "why" of the world for ourselves.

Before you can begin breaking a text down into its component parts, you need to determine what those parts are. Thus your analysis must begin with a close reading of the text itself. When you begin reading a book or a story, you are like a detective who has to be alert for clues even without knowing yet what the mystery is. Because you can't be sure what is important and what isn't, you must treat everything in the text as important—every fact, every detail, every image, every scrap of dialogue. Gradually the smaller parts of the text will begin to arrange themselves into larger parts, and you will begin to see, or at least sense, how these parts are working together to make the text the thing that it is. When you reach that point, you are ready to begin your analysis.

4.3 ■ Preparing To Write the Analysis Essay: Informal Writing Tasks

■ Informal Writing Task 1

Write a summary of the text you plan to analyze. Refer to Chapter 3, section 3.1 for information about how to write an effective summary.

■ Informal Writing Task 2

Develop and answer focusing questions to help you discover and perhaps narrow your topic.

- ◆ What doesn't seem to fit?
- ◆ What details do you notice?
- ◆ What confuses you?
- ◆ What patterns do you notice?
- ◆ What is the overall effect of the text?
- ◆ What made the text easy or difficult to read?
- ◆ What questions does this text raise?
- ◆ What position does this text take?
- ◆ What rhetorical techniques does the text use?
- ◆ What conflicts do you see in the text?

■ Informal Writing Task 3

Develop a working thesis. Most often, the thesis in an analysis essay answers a "how" question. To get started, you might try to answer questions like the following:

- ◆ How does the author use _____ to accomplish _____?
- ◆ How does the text demonstrate _____?
- ◆ How does a particular rhetorical technique affect the success of the text?
- ◆ How does the pattern you found contribute to the meaning of the text?
- ◆ How does the structure affect you as a reader?

■ Informal Writing Task 4

Find textual evidence that supports your answer/thesis. List pieces of potential evidence that you think might support your thesis, including quotations. This detailed textual evidence will provide support for your argument.

Depending on the genre (essay, novel, poem, or story), your textual evidence might include some of the following:

- events
- characters
- setting
- symbols
- significant patterns of action

- patterns of language
- authorial voice
- tone
- statistical data
- direct quotations

Once you have compiled your evidence, you are ready to take that bold step we call the first draft. But if you have completed the four informal writing tasks above, your first draft will hardly be a "rough" one. You will have a good thesis in mind and a good idea of what evidence you will use to support that thesis. In most cases, you will start your paper with your thesis, usually stated as a generalization. Then you will present your specific textual evidence and weave that evidence into a focused, coherent argument.

The sample below illustrates this pattern in a single paragraph, beginning with an abstraction ("foolish devotion") and a generality ("material things") and then providing specific details that bring both the abstraction and the generality to life. This is often how specific textual evidence supports a thesis statement.

Sample Paragraph

In *The Poisonwood Bible,* Barbara Kingsolver suggests that the average American maintains a foolish devotion to material things. This idea is perfectly illustrated by the Price family when they first fly off to Africa. To evade the luggage weight restrictions of the airlines, each of the daughters ends up wearing, as Leah describes it, "six pairs of underdrawers, two half-slips and camisoles; several dresses one on top of the other, with pedal pushers underneath; and outside of everything an all-weather coat" (15). In addition, their pockets and waistbands are stuffed with everything from claw hammers to boxes of cake mix (17). As they disembark in Africa, they literally sag and sweat under their burden—symbolically weighted down by their own materialism. By the end of the book, most of the Prices—no longer "average" Americans—view the easy abundance of America cynically. Adah and Leah are even "secretly scornful" (440) of it, almost ashamed of American supermarkets "where entire shelves boast nothing but hair spray, tooth-whitening cream and foot powders" (441). As Leah's Africa-raised son asks, "But, Aunt Adah, how can there be so many *kinds* of things a person doesn't really need?" (440, 441). *How, indeed,* Kingsolver seems to be saying.

4.4 Readings with Analysis

In this section are two sample *primary texts*—that is, works that are to be the subject of analysis. Each of these primary texts is followed by a faculty-written essay that analyzes the text, much as you will be asked to do.

■ *Fiction:*

◆ The first primary text is a short story called "Signs of Life," by Bob Hicok, who teaches creative writing here at Virginia Tech. The story is about a couple who marry relatively late in life.

◆ Bob's story is then analyzed by Katie Fallon, an instructor of composition and creative writing at Virginia Tech.

■ *Nonfiction:*

◆ The second primary text is an essay called "One of an Army," by Taylor Ahlstrom, who wrote it for an Advanced Composition class at Virginia Tech. It is a thought-provoking consideration of her brother, who has returned from war.

◆ Taylor's essay is analyzed by Sheila Carter-Tod, an assistant professor on the English faculty at Virginia Tech.

4

Signs of Life

by Bob Hicok

Tom held a fluorescent bulb in each hand. They lit up with no wires attached, and Judy walked around him to make sure it wasn't a trick.

"Told you," he said. She was scared of him because shadows moved across his face like the night had become a vampire movie.

"How are you doing that?" she asked. "This can't be real. Light bulbs don't just light up on their own." It was their first date.

"Look." He bobbed his head in the direction of the power grid just beyond the edge of the field. "It's the power lines. They create an electromagnetic field. Can you believe this?" He spun around in a circle until he was dizzy. "Your turn."

"No way," she said. "Just standing here can't be good for us." It was almost mid-
night. They'd been to dinner and a movie. When they drove into the country,
Judy thought he wanted to make out. Even thinking of that expression made her
feel sixteen. She was forty-seven.

"Come on. Just one. We'll each hold one."

"Does it burn?"

"No. You can wear one of my gloves. It'll be fun. You can tell people about the
night you were a lamp. How many people can say that? That they were a human
lamp?"

She liked the human lamp idea. She liked how much he smiled. He was spinning
again. She said yes.

He gave her his left glove. It was too big; it swallowed her hand. When she
picked up the bulb, he held her other hand. They stood there for a long time,
looking at the glow of the city in the distance and the glow in their hands. When
they kissed, their tongues barely touched.

"Is this your usual first date?" she asked.

They got married in a small church a year later. Judy's father gave her away.
Tom's side of the church was empty compared to Judy's, so Judy's family spread
themselves around "like jam," her aunt Lilith said. After they kissed at the end of
the ceremony, Tom and Judy leaned their heads together. People wondered if he
said something romantic. Judy said yes, though she had simply asked him if that
was a new toothpaste and it was. Peppermint.

They were surprised how easily Judy got pregnant, given her age. She started to
worry. She worried about that night in the field. She worried about nuclear
weapons, big ones from the sky and little ones in suitcases. She worried about
mice droppings that carry the Hanta virus, and bats that carry rabies, though
she read that very few bats have rabies. "It's a myth," the author wrote, "perpetu-
ated by our fear of the night." She thought of those filmstrips about mitosis,
cells splitting and multiplying by two over and over, and worried about all the
things that could go wrong as the body grew under the rule of this simple math.
She'd sit in the red chair by the window and look at the trees with green leaves
and later the trees with brown leaves. She'd look at the stars and the sun, at
neighbor kids playing baseball and hitting each other with large, orange bats.
And during all this worrying and watching, she kept her hands across her middle, a middle that grew until she had to walk in a strange way, as a piano would
walk in a cartoon. And she didn't want to eat anymore, but she had to eat. And
she didn't want to go to the bathroom or she wanted to go to the bathroom all
the time. Her middle got so big that it wasn't her body and she could only sleep
in the red chair and then for maybe an hour each night. And during this hour,
she had dreams that the baby had a cheese grater for a head or talked backward
and in one dream a doctor held the baby above her face and told Judy to say
goodbye, that the child was going back to its real mother. After Ellen was born,
Judy's friend Doris asked Judy if she'd do it again.

Judy remembered throwing up and tearing the stitches of her episiotomy. She remembered the Olympic event called "picking up your shoe" and that her breasts were breaking her back. Then she remembered watering a plant or looking at the moon and feeling that inside her was the same thing that makes the sky and oceans work, and she blew on her tea and said to Doris, "yes yes yes."

Tom told her about his heart on their second date. They were at "The Windmill." Tom hit his green ball seven times, and seven times the green ball hit the yellow windmill. Judy made it through on her second try.

"Why are you telling me this?" she asked. "You should be telling me that you're secretly an excellent golfer. Telling me you've got a bad heart . . . that's not a very good sales pitch."

Tom picked up the ball and walked it around to the other side. "I'm telling you because I love you and it's just a matter of time until you love me." He put the ball in front of the cup, lay down and blew it into the hole.

"How much time?" Judy asked. Her hands were on her hips and she was smiling.

"That's up to you, though I'd like you to hurry up. The sooner you love me the sooner we can buy a house and go into debt and stay up putting toys together on Christmas Eve."

"You have a plan."

"Yes. You're the plan." The next hole was "The Dragon."

Not long after Ellen was born, Tom stopped working. He ran out of breath going up the stairs. Judy's mother took care of Tom and Ellen while Judy was at work. His doctor was looking for a new heart, but whenever he talked about the chances of finding a match, Judy noticed his voice got lower.

For a year and a half, Tom spent most of his time in the red chair. He watched Ellen roll around on the ground; then she was crawling; then she was standing like a blade of grass in wind; then she'd run a bit and fall and her eyes would spring open as she tried to choose between giggling and crying; then she was making sounds a river makes and then she was making sounds that wanted to be words and then she said "over" for "Grover" and "sup" for "up," which is what she said when she wanted to be picked up and that's what Tom said when he wanted her to be picked up and brought to him.

"You should have explained about your heart before you did the thing with the light bulbs." They were in bed and wanted to make love, but Judy was afraid he would die during sex. "And don't tell me you'll come as you go. That wasn't funny the first time."

It was Christmas. Their neighbor went crazy each year: Santa with reindeer on the roof; the word NOEL in 8-foot, blinking letters on the front lawn; a nativity scene illuminated by spotlights, as if the arrival of the baby Jesus was a Hollywood

4

premier. The glow from his yard spilled into their room and across their bed. Tom was almost transparent by then; Judy was sure she saw a red glow through his skin.

"So that's why you love me. The light bulbs." This was their ritual. A couple times a year they'd go over that first date. Only this time, Judy came back to what she'd asked him that night.

"Was that just something you did? Was that your move?" She didn't know why it mattered all of a sudden, or why she was sure he'd done the light trick with other women, but if he had, she wanted him to say so.

"Well." He'd been on his back but he turned to face her. "Yeah. I took a few women out there."

"And miniature golf?"

"Some of them, sure. So what?"

She bit his shoulder. "So what?" she said with a hunk of his shoulder in her mouth, the words slurred and tasting of cotton. She bit harder, feeling the give of his flesh, and wanted to bite harder still, until blood, until she could taste what he was inside, until she could swallow him and carry him in her belly and crap him out and be done with him. This feeling passed in a couple seconds, but there was a different kind of time inside those seconds, a slower time, and if she kept biting, if she hung on, she could be mad at him forever, mad in that way that isn't mad, that's love.

"What the hell was that?" he said, rubbing his shoulder. He pulled up the sleeve of his t-shirt and they looked at the impression of her teeth in his skin. "I'm sorry I ever went out with anyone else. I'm sorry anyone else exists. I'm sorry we didn't meet when we were two." Judy thought the teeth looked like a brand and wondered how long it would last.

When he died, people said to Judy, "At least you're prepared." This made her feel another Judy must have stood beside her and that this other Judy went to work and cleaned the house. All the time, there was a noise in the real Judy's head like a rock tumbler, even when she sat at the kitchen table with the lights out. Tom's death wasn't a surprise and she was prepared in the theoretical way people are prepared for dentures or winter. But the first time she made an ice cream cone for Ellen, her daughter ran to the red chair to give her father the first lick. When Judy sat in the chair to talk to Ellen, Ellen slapped her arm and told her to get out.

It was July, one of those blue days, the light porcelain, all the lawns alive with water and kids, music coming from cars and windows, a few clouds on the horizon, the kind that evaporate at the end of the day, cumulus humilis, the words suggesting accumulation and humility.

Ellen was five. Her best friend was Shawna Koop. Shawna had an extra front tooth. The two of them came running into the house and up the stairs. Judy called up after Ellen, who said nothing back.

Judy found Ellen face down on her bed. "What's wrong?" she asked, sitting on the bed and touching her daughter's head. Ellen didn't move.

"We were doing Double Dutch with Cathy and Mary and they said she don't have a daddy and never did and her momma's old and is gonna die and she's gonna be gived away to a home," Shawna said in one breath, her white cheeks turning pink. "I kicked Mary in the knee and we ran," she added.

Judy spooned behind Ellen and hugged her as she cried. Shawna came around the other side of the bed and put Boo, a brown bear with one arm gone, next to Ellen's face. Shawna said she had to go. Ellen and Judy stayed in bed until the long shadows came out. Tom had been dead two years.

Later that night, Ellen put the videotape on the kitchen table. It was unmarked. She kept it in a Derbin's shoe box in the back of her closet, under a pile of books. Tom was on the tape, holding Boo, talking about the time Ellen fell asleep on his stomach, about the yoyo they played with on the bridge in Chicago, about the way she'd pick each piece of cereal out of the milk by hand, about how her lips squished to one side when she concentrated on her coloring, about how she smelled, like flour he said, and later like rain, about when she held her hand out the window of the car and her mother told her not to and he put his hand out too and said that's what cars are for.

He'd asked Judy to go with him and buy a bunch of light bulbs. He wanted to spread them in that field in the shape of the words, I LOVE YOU ELLEN, and Judy would film him standing there. She said it was a terrible idea, that those wires are probably killing people, that everything we do is killing someone, she went on about asbestos and radon and PCBs and cigarettes and guns and how did they know something didn't get into his heart, some virus or bug or toxic goo and he'd be fine if it hadn't, how did they know anything at all anymore about what happens to people? They were both crying by then.

"It's just a bad heart," he said.

Judy knew Ellen wasn't old enough to watch the tape, but she liked touching it. She took it back upstairs and got the stethoscope Tom's doctor had given him. Ellen was in her room reading a book in which a hippo learns to dance. Judy had her come over to her bed. She put the stethoscope on Ellen but left one side off so Ellen could hear her speak.

"This is you," she said, putting the listening other end of the stethoscope to Ellen's chest.

"And this is me," she said, moving it to her chest.

"And anytime you want, you can listen to me or you can listen to you. And anytime I want, I can listen to me or listen to you. How's that?" Judy said, touching Ellen's cheek.

4

"The Night Had Become a Vampire Movie":

The Search for Eternal Youth in
Bob Hicok's "Signs of Life"

by Katie Fallon

Bob Hicok's short story "Signs of Life" explores the relationship between Tom, a miniature-golf aficionado with a bad heart, and Judy, a mother for the first time at age forty-seven. On their first date, Tom takes Judy to a field near a power grid. He impresses her by becoming "a human lamp," holding fluorescent bulbs in both hands that light up with no wires attached; he explains that the power lines "create an electromagnetic field" (69). A year later, the two marry, and in due time Judy gives birth to Ellen, the couple's only child. Tom dies of a "bad heart" when Ellen is three years old. Before Tom dies, he and Judy make a videotape of him to give to their daughter. Even though Ellen "wasn't old enough to watch the tape," touching it gives Judy strength during difficult times (73). "Signs of Life" illustrates the idea that while death will inevitably visit all living things, through a combination of love, imagination, and an understanding of the natural cycles of life, people can learn to accept and, in a sense, overcome their own mortalities. The story also demonstrates the current cultural trend of middle-aged couples becoming first-time parents while it examines mortality's effect on their relationships. Tom and Judy's desire to feel eternally youthful motivates many of their actions, but by the end of the story unfortunate biological realities catch up with them.

Tom and Judy's search for youth becomes apparent during the opening scene. On their first date near the power grid, Judy feels momentarily afraid "because shadows moved across [Tom's] face like the night had become a vampire movie" (69). Seduction and an exchange of blood is an important aspect of most vampire mythology; so is the promise of eternal youth. In traditional vampire tales, the vampire seduces the victim, drinks her blood, and thereby makes the victim immortal like himself. At first, "Judy thought [Tom] wanted to make out. Even thinking of that expression made her feel sixteen" (70). Being with Tom and thinking about potential sexual encounters with him subtracts over thirty years from Judy's age. Her fear of shadows and the health risks they were taking by standing in an electromagnetic field wane by the end of the evening, when Judy and Tom share a kiss. During the kiss, "their tongues barely touched" (70). This event also mirrors an adolescent "make-out" interaction. Judy's suspicions about a vampire movie are fulfilled; in a way, Tom becomes a vampire by making Judy young.

While Judy is pregnant with the couple's child, she spends much of her time reclining in a red chair near a window. She "look[s] at the trees with green leaves and later the trees with brown leaves" (70). Judy observes one of the cycles of nature; in spring and summer, a tree's leaves are new, but later, in autumn, they fade to brown. She is also troubled by disturbing dreams, including one in which the doctor "held the baby above her face and told [her] to say goodbye, that the child was going back to its real mother" (70). Judy realizes that she is not as young as most mothers and experiences anxiety about her baby. Like the leaves, Judy begins to feel that she is fading from summer to autumn; however, she also feels that the baby "inside her was the same thing that makes the sky and oceans work." And she emphatically admits that she would go through the entire experience again (71). Although being pregnant is physically difficult for Judy, it also contributes to her feeling strong and connected to the natural cycles of the rest of the world.

While the birth of their daughter Ellen makes Judy feel younger, it has the opposite effect on Tom. Tom's "bad heart" forces him to stop working shortly after his daughter's birth. The red chair that Judy rested on so often while pregnant becomes the place where Tom "spent most of his time" (71). In much the same way that Judy watched nature grow and change from the chair, Tom watches Ellen "roll around on the ground," then take her first steps, but his health is so poor that Judy is afraid to have sex with him. Once, after a short argument, Judy becomes angry with Tom and bites his shoulder. She "wanted to bite harder still, until blood" (72). Just as Tom had made her younger on their first date, Judy wants Tom to remain young with her forever. Now Judy has become the "vampire," trying to pass immortality on to Tom. Hearts, of course, are filled with blood; vampires need to consume blood in order to remain eternally young. While Judy is biting him, she feels that "if she hung on, she could be mad at him forever, mad in that way that isn't mad, that's love" (72). After she pulls back, the two inspect the bite mark left on his arm, and Judy "wondered how long it would last." The question here is not just how long "the impression of her teeth in his skin" will remain, but how much longer Tom will live (72). This scene reflects the opening scene of the story; Tom succeeded in making Judy younger, and Judy tries to do the same for him.

The fantasy that Judy and Tom will be young and healthy forever together cannot last, and Tom dies when Ellen is three years old. At age five, she is mocked by other children for not having a father and for having a mother who is "old and is gonna die" (73). While eternal biological life may not be possible, Tom manages to live on through technology by making a video for his wife and daughter. On the tape, Tom talks "about the time Ellen fell asleep on his stomach, and the yoyo they played with on the bridge in Chicago," and other events that she is unlikely to remember as she grows older (73). While he may have been unable to retain eternal youth, Tom has, in a way, achieved immortality by preserving his memory for Ellen.

As with all cycles in nature, living organisms are born, grow up, grow older, and eventually die, but like Ponce de Leon, humans have for centuries attempted to subvert this biological rule. In "Signs of Life," Tom and Judy's search for eternal youth is apparent. Tom makes Judy feel like a teen-ager and Ellen's birth strengthens Judy's connection to the world. Unfortunately, the fantasy ends when Tom's "bad heart" catches up with him and he dies. Bob Hicok shows some of the pitfalls of having children later in life, but also illustrates some of the more fulfilling aspects of falling in love and becoming parents, regardless of age. While Tom's "bad heart" prevents him from being young forever, he still manages to find a way to remain eternally alive through and for his daughter. At the end of the story, Judy takes out a stethoscope that Tom used before he died, and together, she and Ellen listen to each other's hearts, to each other's "signs of life."

Work Cited

Hicok, Bob. "Signs of Life." *Composition: Writing, Revising, and Speaking*. Virginia Tech Department of English. Boston: Pearson Custom Publishing, 2005. 69–73.

4

One of an Army

by Taylor Ahlstrom

Walking into Walter Reed Army Hospital, I am overpowered by the sense of life-lessness. My father and I ask for directions to Ward 54 and, after taking several elevators and following endless stretches of numb, white hallways, we arrive at the Psychiatric Ward. We are here to visit my only brother Graham, whom I haven't seen in over six months. My father and I wait for fifteen minutes in a small square room with one fishing magazine while his surprise McDonald's din-ner gets cold. Finally my brother walks in, wearing hospital pajamas and slip-pers. I look into his eyes, which, due to a plethora of daily medications, are glassy and distant. My eyes start to tear up at his condition. My brother is a Sergeant in the United States Army. He spent a period of time in Afghanistan fol-lowing September 11, and another seven-month tour in Iraq during Operation Iraqi Freedom. He has spent more than 80% of his time in the army overseas, including time in Kuwait, Egypt, Kosovo, and Macedonia. On top of two war experiences, he has been stationed in South Korea along the DMZ, supposedly the most dangerous U.S. base in the world. Looking at him now, I can't begin to imagine what he has really been through, or what he has become. All I see before me is a broken man in hideous pajamas.

I close my eyes and think back to the person Graham has always been. Growing up and throughout high school, he consistently threw himself into the spotlight, willing to embarrass himself a bit to get a laugh, and to toss himself onto the mercy of others. His effervescent personality was something I had always admired, and something that without question rubbed off on me over the years. As children we were inseparable, daily playing games of his making. In summer it was always "Spy vs. Spy," the water-gun version of the one-on-one battle of arch nemeses, and in any hotel room, it was always "Crabs," where he would crouch between the two beds and grab at me and my sister's ankles as we strategically jumped across. He was always full of life and excitement, and I find I can no longer focus on a single memory of him, but rather see only a picture: an idea of someone created, but completely intangible. My mind wanders in and out of these distant memories, and slowly I return to the somber reality we are now faced with.

He has been diagnosed with Post-Traumatic Stress Disorder, a condition com-monly found around young men who have been placed into battle. He is on medication to help him sleep and medication to keep him calm, as well as five others whose function neither one of us is sure of at this point. My brother, always a very sensitive man who wrote poetry and was an artist in high school, was put face to face with war and ultimately lost the battle. In the past two years he has constantly regaled the family over holiday meals with stories of living in a tank for sixty days, or hiking for a week with eighty pounds of gear, but today he does not. Today he begs me and my father to find him a way out.

He begs us to get him off the medications that are constantly clouding his head. Suddenly a nurse comes over to me and asks me to put on a hospital gown. After asking why, I learn that some of these men have been in here for years, and the inch of my bare midriff may just put them over the edge. It hits me once again: my brother definitely does not belong here.

My father and I leave the hospital that night pained and confused. Graham didn't know himself what he wanted, and it was pretty obvious that there wasn't anything we could do. I call him a few weeks later, after his in-patient release, only to try to figure out where my one-time idol has gone. What is it that can change a person so much? War is obviously a traumatic experience, yet that day I saw a completely different man before me. Trying to discover who this new man is, I can't help but inquire about the most painful memories he possesses. He tells me that the best way he is dealing with everything is through his groups. He can talk through the experiences and talk to other people who have had similar ones. I ask him to tell me a story. First he speaks of the Apache helicopters. As he and his men were sitting on the Iraqi border, he remembers watching them run their patterns, firing missiles like a broken record. But that, that was nothing compared to the face-to-face. "It would get so close and chaotic, you wouldn't have your gun ready, so you would get into hand-to-hand combat, and then you just had to reach for your knife." As he tells me this, his voice seems relatively emotionless. Perhaps it is the ultimate finality of the whole thing. Perhaps it is the seven medications he is taking daily. We are both silent for a moment, and suddenly the poetic brother I knew five years ago returns. "We were like carpenters. That had never built a house." He pauses thoughtfully for a moment, contemplating the weight of his words. "We learned how to pound the nail into the wood a thousand times, but never knew how to put it all together." We are both silent for a moment again.

His comment brings me back. As he continues speaking, now relating humorous stories of the hospital, I unconsciously drift back into thought. At fourteen I sneaked into his room to steal a cigarette. Lying on the floor in the back of his closet was a thick black journal, a tiny piece of paper marking a page somewhere near the beginning. My insatiable curiosity brought me to open it. This marked the first time I ever saw my brother's artistic side. This book, this mysterious black book, was filled with drawings and poetry, thoughts and experiences. My brother suddenly blossomed into an entirely new dimension. He was hilarious and fun but was also incredibly introverted and sensitive as well. Reading his personal and private thoughts, I suddenly felt as though as I was violating something nestled very deep inside of him, and I left the room with a tang of guilt in my mouth. I never told him I knew about that journal, or even that I knew he wrote such thoughtful poetry. The war had been traumatic, and a simple comment suddenly made me realize that Graham hadn't disappeared, but was just a little scarred from the experience.

Forcibly bringing out the worst of his memories, I can't help but feel that the weight of the war is resting partially on my shoulders now, and I ask what happened to him. What happened in South Korea that had sent him home? Perhaps I can figure out how to explain this half-disaster, half-miracle that no one else has been able to. The war has given him terrible nightmares. He is unable to get any decent amount of sleep. When he does, he pictures himself in battle, and his family watching. They are terribly ashamed at the things he is doing, but he is helpless to stop. He begins to sleep less and less, and eventually becomes more irritable. "It's hyper-vigilance. When you think there is always someone there. You are always suspect. You react harshly. Someone taps you on the shoulder and you put them in a choke hold ready to kill them before you even think to ask them why they're there." He explains this more like a doctor than someone who is living through it, and my mind suddenly jumps to Christmas last year, when over a game of Pictionary he had the most violent attack of rage I had ever seen. He screamed at everyone, yelling bigoted comments and thrashing words around the room. Slowly I was beginning to see exactly what this war had done to him. The bigger question now was how he was going to fix it.

His current plan of action consists of five weekly therapy groups and seven daily medications. These include, as he listed them for me, a generic Prozac for depression and anxiety; Trazodone for depression and sleepless tension; Sertraline for panic attacks, obsessive compulsive disorder and social anxiety; Mirtazapine for depression; Ambien to induce sleep and calm the nightmares; Remeron for hyper-vigilance; and Colopine for shakes and tremors, which he has developed somewhere along the way. Where did he go, that boy? At eighteen, like so many others, wanted to get out of the bubble he was living in. He was scared of college and the real world, but more than that he wanted to see the world and do something big. It just so happened that the something big did him instead.

Graham is now out of Walter Reed's Ward 54 In-Patient program. He has been transferred to the Army Hotel while the barracks are being renovated, and participates daily in the Walter Reed Ward 53 Out-Patient program. As I talk with him on the phone, I ask him how his new treatment is going. "It's going pretty good," he says with the same blind enthusiasm he used to cling to so tightly. "They have me come in a lot, but it's much better than being in there with all the crazies." When I ask him what exactly his treatment is, he starts rolling through his list of weekly therapy sessions: Combat Stress Group, Post-Traumatic Stress Disorder Group, Anger Management Group, and Depression Management Group.

In talking to him, I have trouble discerning whether he is really doing better, or if it's just the medications. He tells me he wishes he could be off them, but he doesn't think he's ready just yet. He sounds like he is struggling with himself a little, but that he knows what he wants, and he does. He's going to get as far away as he can. He will be getting an honorable discharge eventually, and tells me that he never wants to be a part of something so structured again. Despite his positive outlook, I know he is still pained inside. He tells me how for so long he felt no emotion. "You just can't, not when you have to be killing people. Now it's like a whole flood of emotion all at once." I can tell he has been struggling with this, but I decide not to pry any further. He has a lot of anger inside him that I don't think anyone can fix. He has been a compulsive liar for years, though he was nothing but truthful with me. He drinks as often as he can, despite his daily drug regimen. Before I hang up the phone, he says, "Wait. There's one more thing. People should know there isn't one single person fighting over there for Bush or to bring the enemy down, or anything political. They aren't fighting for anything except the guys to the right and left of them. Because if you don't fight, your buddies are gonna die, and that's it."

Graham has always supported the war, and though I never have, he suddenly makes me realize something about every man there. They all just want to come home. This is my brother, and we all know there are thousands more sisters waiting at home all the same. But that isn't what makes him important. He may not have ended up a war hero; more likely, the war killed something inside of him that he can never get back. He is down right now and hurting more than any words of mine can express, but he is on his way back up. Maybe he is just my brother, but to me there is nothing more miraculous than that.

I've read this article to my brother, making sure I have portrayed him accurately. However, after hearing this, he has said that he doesn't want to be considered any kind of miracle. Asked how he would like to be considered, he responded, "Tell them I'm single."

A Reconciliation of the Past, Reality, and Hope

by Sheila Carter-Tod

"One of an Army" is Taylor Ahlstrom's profile of her brother Graham, who is in an army hospital being treated for Post-Traumatic Stress Disorder. Taylor's profile uses the harsh realities of his current situation, woven in with her memories, to help Taylor and the reader come to some understanding of who Graham is. The reader is forced along with Taylor to try to reconcile the contrasting images of Graham as an "effervescent personality [she] . . . always admired" and Graham as "a broken man in hideous pajamas" whom she visits in Walter Reed Hospital with her father (77). Taylor uses stories told by her brother to try to show the reader how he has become who he is. Through the stories she chooses to include, she also reveals as much about her own hopes for him as he does about the horrors that have brought him to his current state. In her attempt to portray Graham accurately, Taylor illustrates, with a child-like hope, that the brother she thought she had and currently has are not in reality who he is. What she actually ends up doing is setting up a series of impressions that she then expands/clarifies/contradicts by presenting more stories—both hers and his. Although not intentionally deceiving the reader, what Taylor does through these stories is to present hopeful misconceptions. Her journey of hope is much like the instinct in all of us to create and hope for a personality in others that can never be a reality because its foundation is riddled with the reality of time and the deceptiveness of our own feelings and memory.

Although she does not present the incidents chronologically, Taylor takes the reader through progressive transformations of her brother, each informed by scenes that show the inherent nature of reality fused with story and memory. The first and most disturbing image of her brother is that of the hospital patient "[w]earing hospital pajamas and slippers [whose] eyes . . . due to a plethora of daily medications, are glassy and distant" (77). Yet it is not just this image of a man broken by war that Taylor wants the reader to have of Graham. Taylor gives the reader a second image of "a very sensitive man, who wrote poetry and was an artist in high school . . . hilarious and fun, but . . . also incredibly introverted[,]" a person who "consistently threw himself in the spotlight, willing to embarrass himself a bit to get a laugh" (77); this is an image she created after searching for cigarettes in her brother's closet and discovering poetry in his journal. To reconcile the images she first presents, Taylor gives the reader the stories that created what she describes as this "half-disaster half-miracle" that no one else has been able to figure out (79). She recounts his telling her stories of Apache helicopters: "As he and his men were sitting on the Iraqi border, he remembers watching them run their patterns, firing missiles like a broken record. But that, that was nothing compared to the face to face" (78). Then using his own words to help us understand what has made him who he is, she quotes him directly: "It would get so close and chaotic, you don't have your gun ready, so you would get into hand-to-hand combat, and then you just have to reach for your knife" (78). This description is further reiterated by his own description of his condition: "It's hyper-vigilance. When you think there is always someone there. You are always suspect. You react harshly. Someone taps you on the shoulder and you put them in a choke hold ready to kill them before you even think to ask them why they're there" (79). But this is not the brother that she knows or wants to accept is there, so she rhetorically questions the situation in an attempt to reconcile the man before her with the man she had thought her brother to have been:

> Where did he go, that boy? At eighteen he, like so many others, wanted to get out of the bubble he was living in. He was scared of college and the real world, but more than that he wanted to see the world and do some-thing big. It just so happened that the something big, did him instead. (79)

Taylor's questions have two effects. First, it would appear that she, too, realizes that the aspects of her brother that she wants to present are far more complicat-ed than she had first realized; second, her questions show her struggle to explain the behaviors she sees in him now that she finds uncharacteristic and in conflict with her image of who her brother is. In reflecting upon what has changed her brother, Taylor complicates the picture both for herself and for the reader by then recounting a disturbing memory:

> . . . my mind suddenly jumps to Christmas last year, when over a game of Pictionary he had the most violent attack of rage I had ever seen. He screamed at everyone, yelling bigoted comments and thrashing words around the room. Slowly I was beginning to see exactly what this war had done to him. (79)

Yet while she comes close to describing her brother as alien, terrifying, and irre-versibly damaged, Taylor permeates her profile with hope until she ultimately sees his transfer to the Walter Reed Ward 53 Out-Patient Program with the same "blind enthusiasm he used to cling to so tightly" (79). Much as a younger sister may look to an older brother to fix or make a situation better, Taylor looks to her brother to make his own situation better. In her statement "[t]he bigger question now, was how he was going to fix it," "it" becomes symbolic of both his current state or condition as well as her image of who he is (79).

By the end of the piece, the reader realizes that Taylor's brother is indeed unable to fix her image of him, or to heal himself, even though Taylor is only beginning to accept their mutual helplessness. In this confused state of both hope and fear—hope that he will eventually, somehow be the brother that she knows and loves, and fear that that brother is gone forever—Taylor complicates the images that she has set out to "accurately" capture throughout the piece by focusing her attentions on who it is that is actually before her now. What she then begins to do—much as she did with her remembrance from Christmas—is to re-create him on her own terms. This re-creation is illustrated by her acceptance that perhaps he won't get better; "I have trouble discerning whether he is really doing better, or if it's just the medications" (79). She further reveals her struggle with the concept of "truth" when she reveals to the reader, "[h]e has been a compulsive liar for years, though he was nothing but truthful with me" (80).

Taylor's attempted reconciliation of the images of who her brother is now with the "effervescent personality [she] . . . always admired" (77) is not a result of her inability to accurately profile Graham; instead, her profile engages the issues of how it is that we know, or can describe, who we think we know and how difficult it is to describe someone we love. In Taylor's profile of her brother, she is not misleading the reader with the paradoxical images she presents of her brother. She is seeking to reconcile past memories of the person she loves with the reality of the person before her. Taylor's hopeful misconceptions are the means by which she pursues this reconciliation of past, present, and hope. Much like the instinct in all of us to somehow stop time and therefore stop the inevitable changes that take place in the lives of our loved ones, Taylor wants to profile the brother she loves and accurately portray him and capture his essence in the process. What she does is to truly capture the nature of any story about someone we love, someone who has been a big part of our lives for a long time. This profile essay is an exercise in the reconciliation of the past, the present, and hope.

Work Cited

Ahlstrom, Taylor. "One of an Army." *Composition: Writing, Revising, and Speaking.* Virginia Tech Department of English. Boston: Pearson Custom Publishing, 2005. 77–80.

4

4.5 Student Examples of the Analysis Essay

Name: Lynnette Hill

Hometown: Winchester, Virginia

Major: Political Science

Last book read for fun: *Jonah's Gourd Vine* by Zora Neale Hurston

Favorite on-campus spot: The Pylons and the Chapel

Advice for other students in first-year composition class:
When writing journals, take the writing seriously because journal writing helps you learn what your thoughts are and what is important to you. Also, I had not thought about allowing another individual to comment on my paper because I believed that it would take away from the creativity in the paper. I now know that the help of another individual is extremely beneficial to my writing because it allows me to see what is and is not necessary in my paper without destroying my creative thoughts/ideas.

What stood out for you about your first English class at Tech?
As a first-year English student at Tech, I learned that there are multiple options available to me when I need extra help writing or simply organizing my thoughts.

The student comments on the writing process:

Kathy Combiths and her student Lynnette Hill

When writing this essay, I explored writing through first placing myself in the essay and visualizing the events as they occurred. This innovative writing process made analysis come more easily to me. The difficulty appeared when I had too many interesting and innovative thoughts that I felt should be included in the paper. It is some-times hard for me to purge ideas that I think everyone would find interesting. I also experienced difficulty in elaborating too much on one idea and losing focus of the main topic of the essay. Through revision, I learned that when I focused too much on the essay as a whole, I often overlooked the small things, such as transitions between sentences and ideas as well as grammar issues.

Lynnette Hill
Instructor: Katherine Combiths
English 1105 Analysis I
September 19, 2004

Looking Beyond La isla

"Silent Dancing" by Judith Ortiz Cofer recounts a moment in Cofer's life captured on a home movie as well as many of her childhood experiences growing up as a Puerto Rican and absorbing the American culture in Paterson, New Jersey. Through the use of vivid sensory details, Cofer brings the scene in the home movie to life. The tone of Cofer's essay flows clearly so that the reader does not associate her with someone who is not articulate in the English language. At the same time, Cofer's use of Spanish words and phrases clearly illustrates that she has not forgotten her Puerto Rican roots; as the editors note, "'Silent Dancing' focuses on the way imported cultural values affected the lives of Puerto Ricans" (DiYanni and Hoy 144). Cofer's essay focuses on how American culture impacts the lives of Puerto Ricans; moreover, it also takes a deeper look into how the traditional roles of Puerto Ricans are affected by American culture.

In Hispanic culture, the male is often viewed as the dominant, domineering figure who runs the household, and this dominance is an important value of Hispanic culture. The male is the one who upholds the traditions and keeps everything in order in the household. Born and raised in Puerto Rico, Cofer's father had an obligation to uphold this rich tradition. Upon arriving in America, he realized that things would not be easy for him due to his racial identity. He was denied a home for his family because he was not Jewish, and the house was in a predominately Jewish neighborhood. This experience was an eye-opener for him because with each step he took forward, he took two steps backward in trying to achieve his goals. In response to the setbacks he faced as a Puerto Rican, he decided to change his lifestyle and his traditions to fit the new American culture. He ordered his wife to shop at the supermarket for their food rather than at the Hispanic store, La Bodega, and to disassociate herself from other Puerto Ricans in El Building, which was the apartment complex where they lived. His purpose was to rise up from the stagnant position he had in life and achieve his goals as well as to give his family a better life. As long as he remained in *el barrio,* he would never have the opportunity to rise up from poverty; therefore, he learned to live as an American.

While Cofer's father assimilated into American society, her mother remained secluded by hiding behind the walls built up by her racial and cultural identity. In the Puerto Rican tradition, it is common for the women to submit to their husbands. Cofer's mother was compelled to do as her husband wished. With these constraints, however, she found time to reconnect with her Puerto Rican roots. Although "she liked to buy her dresses at the women's specialty shops like Lerner's and Diana's," she still loved to linger in La Bodega, "for it was there that Mother breathed best, taking in the familiar aromas of the foods she knew from Mamá's kitchen. It was also there that she got to speak to the other women of El Building" (147).

Similar to Cofer's experience, my childhood is filled with memories of my mother's womanly strength and perseverance. As a child, I watched my mother work day and night to be the model preacher's wife. Her allure was not in the clothes she wore or in the things she said but, rather, in the way she presented herself to others. From her smile to the way she dressed, everything about my mother was polished. She realized that my father's success in the ministry depended partly upon her demeanor as the first lady of the church and the upbringing of her children. With this in mind, she kept the family closely-knit, as if we were another patch in a patchwork quilt. Cofer's mother, much like my own mother, had a commitment to her husband to keep their family united. As Americans, they had more opportunities and more chances to attain their goals; therefore, she remained obedient so that this transition into the American society would be as painless as possible.

In the home movie that Cofer narrates, there are three women dressed in red, sitting on a couch at a party. One of the women is *la novia*, or the girlfriend, of her cousin's brother, one is her own mother, and the other woman is *la prima*, her eighteen-year-old cousin. *La novia* had just arrived from Puerto Rico, "which is apparent in her body language. She sits up formally, her dress pulled over her knees" (146). It is obvious from Cofer's description of *la novia* that this woman is completely unfamiliar with American culture. She lowers her eyes when she approaches the camera and, from Cofer's description, remains in the background of the party, not interacting with anyone. Cofer's aunt realizes *la novia*'s humble presence and states, "If he marries her quickly, she will make him a good Puerto Rican-style wife, but if he waits too long, she will be corrupted by the city" (150). This statement describes the opinions of many women in the Puerto Rican culture. During Cofer's childhood, it was essential for the wife of a Puerto

Rican man to be obedient and to be respectful of her husband's wishes because Puerto Rican women were *humilde* and submissive. Like many other women who had just arrived from *la isla, la novia* remains isolated, pining for the day when she will get her chance to return to all that is familiar to her. She is not used to women who are so outspoken, as her future sister-in-law appears to be. The unfamiliar American traditions lead her to cling even more tightly to her Puerto Rican traditions rather than attempting to feel her way through the dark void created when the American and the Puerto Rican cultures meet.

While   portrayed the ideal Puerto Rican woman, *la prima* was an American girl: "She doesn't have a trace of what Puerto Ricans call la mancha (literally, the stain: the mark of the new immigrant—something about the posture, the voice, or the humble demeanor that makes it obvious to every-one the person has just arrived on the mainland)" (146). The dress she is wearing in the home movie is "a tight, sequined, cocktail dress. Her brown hair has been lightened with peroxide around the bangs, and she is holding a cigarette expertly between her fingers, bringing it to her mouth in a sen-suous arc of her arm as she talks animatedly" (146–7). Everything about her bold demeanor screams American. Nothing about her hairstyle or the way she presents herself says that she is Puerto Rican. From her persona, one can see that she has dismissed the traditional Puerto Rican lifestyle and immersed herself in American culture in order to deal with a new country, a new language, and a new way of living life. Rather than growing to be *humilde,* or humble, she chooses to walk down a separate path into the unknown, believing that this path will somehow fulfill her desire to live life as she pleases.

Cofer's mother, who sat in between *la prima* and *la novia,* represented a mixture of the two women. Although she lived an "Americanized" lifestyle, which included shopping at the supermarket, buying clothes from specialty stores, and dining at Woolworth's, she never lost a sense of where she came from. One can best describe Cofer's mother's life as baking a cake with a new recipe; while one uses new ingredients, there still is room for the old ingredi-ents. She never considered turning her back on *la isla;* she simply made room in her life for the two cultures to coexist. Cofer's mother's response is a typical response to the sudden change in lifestyles. Many immigrants rea-soned that it would be best to remember where they had come from, while at the same time they learned more about where they were going.

4

The integration of a person's native culture into American culture is a common occurrence in this country. This concept seems simple, but it really is not. The concept involved Cofer's parents being comfortable with themselves enough to realize that they needed to step outside of the boundaries established by both American and Puerto Rican cultures in order to attain their goals in life. They had to pick out elements of each culture and incorporate them into their lives. Thus, they would be shopping in areas of Paterson, New Jersey, where their family was the only group of Hispanics within miles. As a result, Cofer's family would not be able to connect with all of the other Puerto Rican families living around them in El Building and their home would be the only home filled with the aroma of pine needles on Christmas day. These aspects of their lives set them apart from everyone else in El Building, in the neighborhood, and in their family because it was *una mezcla,* or a mix, of both cultures.

The point that Cofer is trying to make in writing this essay is that her way of living in America is what identifies her. She did not reject her favorite television shows, "Father Knows Best," "The Donna Reed Show," "Leave It To Beaver," "My Three Sons," and "Bachelor Father," nor did she give up eating "meat and plantain pastels, as well as ubiquitous rice made special with pigeon peas—gandules—and seasoned with precious sofrito sent up from the Island" (149). Her father showed her what American culture had to offer her, which he strongly believed was a better opportunity. On the other hand, her mother showed her that her culture was rich and unique in its own way. Nothing that America offered could or would replace the home-cooked Puerto Rican meals with only the best ingredients or the music that spoke to the hearts of her mother and her relatives. This is the very essence of Cofer's identity; she is the culmination of Puerto Rican as well as American elements. Cofer does not clearly state that both cultures define who she is, but it is evident that she would not be the person she is today without the influences from both cultures.

Works Cited

Cofer, Judith Ortiz. "Silent Dancing." *Encounters: Essays for Exploration and Inquiry.* Comp. and ed. Robert DiYanni and Pat C. Hoy II. Boston: McGraw-Hill, 2000. 144–52.
DiYanni, Robert and Pat C. Hoy II, eds. Headnote to "Silent Dancing." *Encounters: Essays for Exploration and Inquiry.* Boston: McGraw-Hill, 2000. 144.

The Instructor Responds:

For the analysis essay, students were asked to analyze Judith Ortiz Cofer's "Silent Dancing" by considering the elements of language and theme in relation to the theme of our class: finding identity through cultural heritage from family, community, and American cultural diversity. In her analysis of Cofer's family's experience as Puerto Rican immigrants and the difficulties involved in their assimilation, Lynnette Hill clearly states her intention to discuss the impact that American culture has on the traditional family roles of other cultures.

Lynnette discusses the roles of the family members by comparing their experiences with the new American culture. She backs up her observations with vivid details from the essay that capture the author's vivid, descriptive language. Her creative style as well as the personal experience that she relates concerning the roles in her own family add to her analysis. She also effectively returns to the thesis of the essay from her personal story. The essay ends with Lynnette's analysis coming to a reasonable conclusion of her discussion in which she makes an assumption about the author's ability to find a sense of identity in her cultural assimilation.

— *Kathy Combiths*

4

Name: Douglas Segal

Hometown: Bridgewater, New Jersey

Major: Computer Engineering

Last book read for fun: *Be Here Now* by Ram Dass

Favorite on-campus spot: The horticulture gardens

Advice for other students in first-year composition class: Enjoy.

What stood out for you about your first English class at Tech?
It was my smallest class, so participation and knowing people's names was a possibility.

The student comments on the writing process:

The thing I enjoyed about this essay was that I was able to be creative and explore new territory where I normally would not have gone. The idea of the bridge was interesting to come up with and then find over and over in the text. As for physically writing the essay, I started out by just freewriting the entire essay with no real planning. From there I went back line by line several times to make sure every sentence had a purpose and that the essay flowed throughout.

Jennifer Lawrence and her student Doug Segal

Doug Segal
Instructor: Jennifer Lawrence
ENGL 1105 Analysis I
October 6, 2004

The Bridge Between

The Woman Warrior by Maxine Hong Kingston is a nontraditional
memoir because of its inclusion of fictional elements. Kingston is also difficult to classify, and from the vantage point of a Chinese-American she
writes about her experiences feeling more like the hyphen between the two
cultures than fitting securely in either. At times unsure of what to believe
and how to live, she writes that first generation Americans "have had to figure out how the invisible world the emigrants built around [their] child-
hoods fits in solid America" (5). As her mother imposes her Chinese culture,
American culture is also being forced upon her, particularly in school.
Kingston is left bouncing from side to side in a constant struggle.
Eventually, she becomes tired of her passive mode and decides, through her
art, to stand firmly in the middle. Throughout her memoir, but particularly
in the last section, "A Song for a Barbarian Reed Pipe," Maxine Hong
Kingston records her life struggle to find a balance between the two cul-
tures of her Chinese past and her American present.

Kingston's awkward position is demonstrated in a scene involving a
wrong delivery from the drugstore, when a delivery boy mistakenly delivers
another family's medicine to Kingston's house. Kingston sees this just as a
simple error, but her mother believes a great curse has been placed upon the
family. Her mother, raging in anger, tells her, "You go to the drugstore. [. . .]
Go and make them stop the curse" (170). Kingston's mother believes in the
power of curses and their ability to destroy families, while Kingston thinks
this belief is ridiculous, and tells her, "There are no such things as curses.
They'll think I'm crazy" (170). This disagreement reveals a clash between the
mother's traditional Chinese views and her daughter's modern American
ones. Kingston, in a sense, must now bridge the cultures to make her
mother happy. "You just translate," her mother tells her (170).

Kingston goes to the drugstore and her intuitions come true: the druggist does not understand the situation and she ends up feeling bad about
the whole ordeal. When she attempts to explain her request for candy to the
druggist, she struggles to speak: "My mother said you have to give us candy.

She said that is the way the Chinese do it" (170). The druggist does not comprehend what Kingston is attempting to say. He tries to offer her some money, and then finally gives her candy. When Kingston returns with candy, her mother is pleased and mocks Kingston's hesitation towards the situation by saying to her, "See? [. . .] They understand. You kids just aren't very brave" (171). Of course Kingston is sure the druggist completely misunderstood, and as she sheepishly recalls with shame, he "thought we were beggars without a home who lived in back of the laundry" (171). In this incident Kingston fails to find a resolution of the two cultures; between her mother's delusion, the druggist's confusion, and Kingston's awkward position, the situation is far from balanced.

Kingston also finds being in school difficult, where she is often not able to speak up, and since "the other Chinese girls did not talk" she knows her inability to communicate has to do with being Chinese (166). In one scene she takes out some of her anger on a quiet Chinese girl at school. She attacks those qualities she shares with the girl, showing her own frustration with those parts of herself: "I hated her when she was the last chosen for her team and I, the last chosen for my team. I hated her China doll hair cut. I hated her at music time for the wheezes that came out of her plastic flute" (173). Both girls rarely talk, both get picked last for teams, both are Chinese. For Kingston, it is the extreme of staring herself down in the mirror. She begins by telling the silent girl, "You're going to talk" (175), but by the end of the ordeal it is not the girl who speaks but Kingston, who has done more talking in this scene than she has up to this point in the book altogether. When Kingston pulls at the girl's hair the girl finally begins to cry, and Kingston herself begins to break down. "Why won't you talk?" she cries (180). She begins trying to rationalize her actions, saying, "I'm trying to help you out [. . .] Don't you ever want to be a cheerleader? Or a pompon girl? [. . .] [Y]ou are a plant. Don't you know that? That's all you are if you don't talk" (180). While Kingston attacks the girl for being "a plant," she knows she will never be a "cheerleader" or "pompom girl" either, but unlike the silent girl, who seems content, Kingston is angry about her position. This event demonstrates her frustration in understanding the quiet girl, herself, and her role as a Chinese-American.

Kingston is in a difficult spot because she not only feels out of place in white American society but detached from her Chinese heritage as well. She finds most of the Chinese traditions unnecessarily secretive and without much meaning, such as her mother's belief that they should bang pots during the eclipse in order to "scare the frog from swallowing the moon" (169). Kingston writes, "When we had not banged lids at the last eclipse and the shadow kept receding anyway, [my mother had] said, 'The villagers must be banging and clanging very loudly back home in China'" (169). When she and her siblings respond, "On the other side of the world, they aren't having an eclipse, Mama. That's just a shadow the earth makes when it comes between the moon and the sun" (169), their mother sees it as them taking the western view and quips, "You're always believing what those Ghost Teachers tell you. Look at the size of the jaws!" (169). While at school Kingston's role is that of being one of the silent Chinese girls (166); at home she becomes one of the Americans, or as her mother refers to them, ghosts. In this way she is caught in the middle of the two cultures, unable to find a sense of belonging in either one.

By the end of her memoir, Kingston has had time to distance herself from her mother and grow independently as a person. This distance helps her figure out how "the invisible world the emigrants built around [her] childhood fits into solid America" (5). However, in the conclusion of the memoir Kingston returns to her roots in her mother's Chinese talk stories and combines a talk story with one of her own. Her mother's story is about Kingston's grandmother who "loved the theater" (196). She enjoyed it so much that she would buy up entire sections of seats for the whole family, but the family worried that if they all were at the play the bandits would rob their unguarded house. To this the grandmother replies, "So let them. [. . .] Leave the house wide open. [. . .] We are going to the theatre with no worries" (207). Ironically, the bandits storm the theater, but the family is left unharmed. The grandmother sees this event as a lesson to always go to plays so the family will be safe from thieves. Her mother reports, "They went to many plays after that" (207). Similarly, Kingston uses art in the form of writing in order to create a safe place for herself.

Kingston extends the metaphor further, by imagining that "at some of those performances, they heard songs of Ts'ai Yen" (207). She proceeds to tell the story of Ts'ai Yen, a young poet who was captured by barbarians and eventually made her home with them. While with the barbarians Ts'ai Yen heard the sounds of war, which were the sounds the barbarians' arrows made when soaring through the air. Kingston writes that at first to the young poet they sounded like "death sounds" (208), but "one night she heard music tremble and rise like desert wind" (208). The sound inspired her to combine the two cultures through song, and sing songs with Chinese words based on the music of the arrows. Her children, who were barbarians and spoke no Chinese, learned the songs and began singing them. Kingston writes, "Her words seemed to be Chinese, but the barbarians understood their sadness and anger. Sometimes they thought they could catch barbarian phrases about forever wandering" (209), demonstrating the synthesis she is able to create between the Chinese and Barbarian language. The songs spread quickly, including back to her native culture, where one became "a song that Chinese sing to their own instruments" (209), completing the circle connecting the culture of the Barbarians with that of the Chinese. Maxine Hong Kingston and Ts'ai Yen both use their art to bridge the gap between cultures; Ts'ai Yen finds her voice in singing her songs and Kingston finds her voice through her writing. In the memoir Kingston asserts that the song of the poet Ts'ai Yen, like her own work, "translated well" (209).

Unable to find resolution during childhood, Kingston demonstrates that with the wisdom of age and a clear mind she is able to discover that balance that she was striving to find, although she also admits that she continues "to sort out what's just my childhood, just my imagination, just my family" (205). Just as Ts'ai Yen finds her voice in song where it becomes a mixture of her two cultures, Maxine Hong Kingston finds her voice in words and stories, using both her past and present. In finding this voice of translation, Kingston discovers that she need not be pulled from culture to culture, but that she may walk the bridge between.

Work Cited

Kingston, Maxine Hong. *The Woman Warrior: Memoirs of a Girlhood Among Ghosts.* New York: Vintage, 1976.

The Instructor Responds:

For the analysis, I asked students to write an essay that examined a cross-cultural aspect of Maxine Hong Kingston's unconventional memoir *The Woman Warrior*. Because the memoir is separated into five distinct sections, I encouraged students to focus on just one section and to choose just one distinct idea to work with within that section. Although students initially protested that their ideas would be too narrow, once they started locating evidence, the text itself demonstrated many ways to strengthen and further develop their original idea. This process resulted in more "stuff to write about" than most students could even fit into a short analysis.

Doug's essay is an example of how this process can work beautifully. He analyzes just four scenes in the section "Song for a Barbarian Reed Pipe" which demonstrate a key aspect of Kingston's memoir—her position as a Chinese-American, and her ongoing internal struggle resulting from this position. He ends his essay by showing how Kingston is able to build a "bridge between" her two often conflicting and confusing cultures through her art.

As Doug's examples build upon each other he shows the complexity of the text, resulting in an essay that is multi-faceted but also unified. I enjoyed reading his essay and also working with him in the revision process, in which he tried to strengthen the connections he was making between each example and his main idea, as well as distinguish between them. I can still see places in which he could further his analysis, but that is often what strong writing does—opens more doors than it closes.

— *Jennifer Lawrence*

Name: John Cosimano

Hometown: Virginia Beach, Virginia

Major: Biology

Last book read for fun: *The Daily Show with Jon Stewart Presents America (The Book): A Citizen's Guide to Democracy Inaction* by the writers of *The Daily Show,* Jon Stewart

Favorite on-campus spot: Lane Stadium — North End Zone

Advice for other students in first-year composition class:
Take your professor's advice on your writing in stride, and don't be afraid to be unique or adventurous.

What stood out for you about your first English class at Tech?
How good the professor (Mrs. LoMascolo) was and how interesting the Arthurian Legend could actually be to write about.

The student comments on the writing process:

*Alice LoMascolo and
her student John Cosimano*

I came up with the idea for the essay easily because I enjoy analyzing and writing about symbolism, and in the selection I read symbolism was very prevalent. The biggest struggle I encountered, which is usually the main struggle I face in all my essays, was the introduction. I spend almost as much time on the title and introduction as I do on the rest of the paper (on a paper this length). If you write a good introduction, the paper will write itself, and it is also the best way to get yourself and others interested in your paper. Finding points, proving them, and explaining yourself is simple enough, but to outline your paper in one paragraph in a way that is not only thorough, but intriguing and exact, is always the most exciting challenge for me as a writer. Through revision I learned that there is always work to be done, and there is always something you will not realize when revising the paper yourself. Getting experienced outside criticism is so important when you're growing as a writer. You learn from your mistakes . . . and you learn to make new ones!

John H. Cosimano
Instructor: Alice LoMascolo
English 1106 Analysis II
7 September 2004

Clothes and the Lack Thereof
(An Essay on Innocence)

Germaine Greer once wrote, "innocence is the denial of life." Conversely, it could be said that experience, or more deviously, corruption, is the method by which one is introduced to true living. Throughout literature this view is echoed by authors who write about a loss of innocence, and in many cases they use symbols to enhance their view. One specific selection of literature in which symbolism related to this theme is undeniable is "Loss of Innocence," a group of stories collected in *Folk and Fairy Tales* of different versions, both early and contemporary, of the famous story of "Little Red Riding Hood." In three particular stories in this collection, the authors use clothes to symbolize innocence and their removal to symbolize a transition into a more mature state.

The anonymously authored "The Story of Grandmother" is one of the oldest versions of the "Red Riding Hood" tale, and it gives an excellent example of clothes being a symbol for innocence. In this version the wolf consumes the grandmother and awaits the arrival of the little girl. Upon arrival, the little girl, unbeknownst to her, is told to consume the flesh and blood of her grandmother. The wolf then tells the girl to rid herself of her clothes: "Where should I put my skirt?" she asks; the wolf replies, "throw it in the fire, my child; you don't need it anymore" (2). This shows that the clothes symbolize innocence because when the little girl eats the flesh and blood of her own grandmother she obviously becomes tainted, and she then removes her clothes. The removal of clothes signifies the loss of innocence of the little girl, piece by piece. The wolf does not actively participate in the removal of the girl's clothes, and this fact demonstrates the independent nature of a loss of innocence. Though he is at fault, he does not force the flesh and blood on the girl, and he does not force the removal of her clothes. Another important aspect of this symbol is that the girl throws the clothes in the fire. This action illustrates that the loss of innocence is permanent, and it cannot be retrieved with simple apology or regret. Finally, the girl escapes the wolf through the use of her wit. She proclaims, "Oh, Grandmother, I need to go outside to relieve myself" (2). This shows that the loss of naïvety accompanies the loss of innocence; her deception enables the girl to flee to safety. In "The Story of Grandmother," the girl loses her clothes to symbolize her permanent loss of innocence and transition from a naïve little girl to a clever young lady.

This symbol remains constant in Charles Perrault's more famous story "Little Red Riding Hood," but Perrault uses it differently, and although the telling of the story changes from the previous account, the symbol remains universal. In this story the wolf again consumes the grandmother and awaits the young girl. She arrives and voluntarily removes her clothes: "Little Red Riding Hood took off her clothes and went to lie down in the bed" (4). The voluntary removal of clothes does not signify a voluntary loss of innocence in this case, but it does symbolize the eventual loss. In this version the wolf is most likely a metaphor for a pedophile, and with that the girl entering the bed will result in her loss of innocence. "At that, the wicked wolf threw himself upon Little Red Riding Hood and gobbled her up, too," Perrault writes (5). However unfortunate and inappropriate the loss may be, it does occur. When a young girl is molested or taken advantage of, her innocence is taken by her attacker, with or without consent. This unfortunate turn of events for Little Red Riding Hood utilizes the clothing as a symbol for innocence in a completely different manner than in the previous version.

Angela Carter's telling of the famous tale, "The Company of Wolves," is a renovation of sorts. It modernizes and revises the traditional story with sexual imagery and a fierce tone that Carter sets from the beginning; however, the use of clothes to symbolize innocence remains the same and is actually strengthened with Carter's newly added twists. Carter discusses clothes in this version with more depth than any of the others, and the reader can easily see how the clothes symbolize innocence. The story describes werewolves in detail with examples and small tales. The werewolf and the little girl figure prove the symbol in this story. "Seven years is a werewolf's natural span, but if you burn his human clothing you condemn him to wolfishness for the rest of his life" (10). Once again the burning of the clothes symbolizes a permanent loss of innocence, but this time it is associated with the wolf, whose state of innocence is equivalent to being human. Human beings, on the other hand, whether male or female, experience a different loss of innocence in the story. The human loss of innocence is one based more strongly on sex in this adaptation than the others.

The loss of innocence in this more modern adaptation of the Red Riding Hood tale is a more sexual kind, and it is one that adds another dimension to the continuing theme. The boy in the story, who is a werewolf, undresses himself in preparation for killing the grandmother: "He strips off his shirt [. . .] the last thing the old lady saw in all this world was a young man [. . .] naked as stone" (12). The loss of clothes here parallels the loss of innocence in the boy as he transforms into the vicious wolf. He then replaces his clothes and returns to his human, innocent form, almost too easily: "when he had finished with her, he licked his chops and quickly dressed himself again, until he was just as he had been when he came through the door" (12). Though it is impossible to regain one's innocence, the boy cloaks his loss of innocence and his true self with the clothes. When the girl arrives at the house, the reader is once again able to see that the clothes symbolize innocence. The girl, who is aware of the danger, is told to throw her clothes in the fire by the boy; just like the wolf in "The Story of Grandmother," the boy says, "throw [the shawl] on the fire, dear one. You won't need it again" (12). The fire foreshadows the permanent loss of innocence that will take place, but Carter adds an unexpected twist that strengthens the symbol when she has the girl voluntarily remove the boy's clothes: "She laughed at him full in the face, she ripped off his shirt for him and flung it into the fire, in the fiery wake of her own disclosed clothing" (13). This powerful imagery reinforces the symbol that proves the permanent, voluntary, and extreme loss of innocence of the girl. She "ripped off" his clothes to show that not all losses are a shame, but it shows that some are liberating experiences. Carter's "The Company of Wolves" adds a new dimension to the idea of a loss of innocence, but it keeps clothes as a symbol for the change, whether it is forced or voluntary.

"Loss of Innocence" is a fitting name for this collection of Red Riding Hood tales because they all involve the tainting, corruption, or liberation of their characters. "The Story of Grandmother," "Little Red Riding Hood," and "The Company of Wolves" all use clothes as a symbol for innocence, and all three stories portray the loss of innocence in a unique manner. If "Innocence is the denial of life," then these Red Riding Hood tales are full of life, after they are stripped down and the reader is able to analyze their symbols.

Work Cited

Hallett, Martin and Barbara, eds. *Folk & Fairy Tales*. 2nd ed. Ontario: Broadview, 1996.

The Instructor Responds:

The course theme was Writing across Cultures and the focus of this 1106 class was on myth and legend. We began the semester by reading different versions of the "Red Riding Hood" tales to search for meaning beyond what was obvious. John became interested in the symbolism of clothing in these tales: What was behind the removal of the clothing, not only of Red Riding Hood but also of the wolf? His deep analysis of this symbol reflects that interest.

John's intriguing quotation by Germaine Greer leads to a strong defensible thesis. The older versions of this tale (as well as Angela Carter's twentieth-century version) reveal topics that might not be considered acceptable bedtime fare for small children. John illustrates the deeper meanings in these tales through the shedding of clothes as symbolic of the shedding of innocence. His main points are supported by effectively chosen quotes, which he discusses and analyzes fully. A particularly significant example is in his discussion of Carter's "The Company of Wolves," when he discusses Red Riding Hood discarding her own clothes then removing the wolf's clothing. He emphasizes her readiness to leave the innocent virginal stage of life when she rips off the wolf's clothing "to show that not all losses are a shame [. . .] some are liberating experiences."

John enjoys the writing process and writes as he might speak in conversation; the result is clear and concise prose leading to a smooth style that is a pleasure to read. John's wit and sense of humor are always subtly interjected into his writing. He enjoys playing with words, which is a sign of competence and confidence in writing, evidenced by the title and last sentence of this essay where the symbols are "stripped down" for the reader to analyze.

— *Alice LoMascolo*

Name: Andrew Long

Hometown: Pulaski, Virginia

Major: Biology

Last book read for fun: *Fear and Loathing in Las Vegas* by Hunter S. Thompson

Favorite on-campus spot: Torgersen Hall 1st Floor

Advice for other students in first-year composition class:
Try not to become stressed out when you work on a paper because that makes your writing seem too forced. Just relax and write what you truly feel about a topic. I wish I had budgeted more time for revising the papers I wrote in English. I realize now that revision, for me, is the most essential part of composing a piece of writing, and I feel my writings could have been greatly improved with a little more revision.

What stood out for you about your first English class at Tech?
The floor was always open for discussion about anything at all. That made the class much more relaxed than any English class I had taken previously.

4

The student comments on the writing process:

Gyorgyi Voros and her student Drew Long

I spent a great deal of time brain-storming for this paper. I believe in spending time carefully working through the prewriting process, because it is the best way to form a unified thesis and continually support that thesis throughout an essay. Even a basic method of categorizing ideas before starting to draft a paper greatly cuts down on the time spent in composition, because every thought that needs to be expressed in the essay is already written down. No time is lost to looking for ways to "beef up" the writing once a draft has been started.

Drew Long
Instructor: Gyorgyi Voros
English H1204 Analysis II
September 21, 2004

The Unity of the Man and the Boat
in Thomas Cole's *The Voyage of Life*

The Voyage of Life, a series of paintings by Thomas Cole, chronicles a man's journey through life. The paintings are entirely metaphorical and serve as a religious allegory, displaying the role of God in the lives of men. The four paintings, *Childhood, Youth, Manhood,* and *Old Age,* depict a man in a boat from infancy to the end of life on an ever changing river. Along the way, an angel is frequently pictured giving advice or guiding the course of the boat, and the sky, or a portion of it, is displayed in a wondrous and holy fashion, marking it as the domain of heaven. The use of water as a metaphor for life is an idea dating back to ancient times, and the notion of angels and a heaven existing in the firmament can be traced to the earliest history. What is it that makes Cole's paintings unique? What inspires their poignancy and value? In *The Voyage of Life* Thomas Cole utilizes light and shadow, common aging patterns, and an absence of action on the part of the man to indicate a unity between the figure of the man and the figure of the boat, a unity that further emphasizes his point that the journey of life, though difficult and fulfilled only at great cost to the journeyer, is guided by and imbued with a sense of a higher power and, ultimately, is beautiful.

To determine the meaning and import of Cole's paintings, one must first place those paintings in the context of who Thomas Cole was and what he believed in and stood for. Cole was most prolific at painting American landscapes. His paintings emphasize the spiritual importance of the American wilderness, a wilderness that was quickly disappearing during his career. Biographer Christy Delafield observes that "In his 'Essay on American Scenery' Cole praises the value of landscape itself, extolling the spirituality inherent in the beauty of scenery. Nature was inseparable from religion, according to Cole. He himself was active in the Episcopal Church" (Delafield). Cole's works are reflections of his belief in the evidence of God in the natural world, and this is likely most true of his religious allegories such as *The Voyage of Life.* This point is important because it allows one to make inferences from *The Voyage of Life* through the lens of Christianity. This governing principle over the four paintings lends coherence to assumptions about the unity of man and boat that must be understood to weave the significance of that unity into the overall meaning behind the paintings.

Throughout the series, Cole uses two obvious techniques to signify a oneness between the man and the boat. First, in all four paintings man and boat are depicted together. This observation is certainly not evidence in itself that the two represent one entity, but it is central to the idea that they do. Secondly, the man is always facing the bow of the boat. This position indicates a union of direction and purpose between the man and the boat. A shared purpose and direction is important for any unit comprised of component parts. For instance, an army, though made up of many individuals, is unified by the direction given by its commander and the purpose of serving and protecting the nation, organization, or idea it was created to serve. The man and the boat in *The Voyage of Life* could be considered an army commanded by God or the angelic figure in the paintings and created to serve the journey or perhaps the man himself. However, more implicit ideas expressed in the paintings suggest a much greater and more encompassing union between the man and the boat.

Cole makes excellent use of the artistic elements of light and shadow to suggest unity between the man and the boat in *The Voyage of Life.* In each of the four paintings, light is cast directly on the man and the boat and, specifically, on the figure affixed to the front of the boat. Artistically, this technique serves to focus the viewer's attention on the boat and figure therein, but the technique also has profound metaphorical implications as well. Light is often associated with the presence of God and the salvation that comes to Christians through Jesus Christ. This use of lighting is Cole's way of depicting God's guidance and direction over the man at every stage in his life. The figure on the bow of the boat is a representation of the man's moral compass. It is most illuminated by the light because Cole believed that a man's moral nature is the greatest indicator of his salvation. In each painting, the figure gives off a golden glow; gold is a color associated with salvation. In *Childhood,* the man emerges from the cave guided by the angel. This is an allegory for baptism, when a young Christian first receives the promise of salvation but must be guided by other believers until such time as he or she can begin interpreting heavenly guidance alone in the salvation of Jesus Christ. *Youth* shows the man drifting into calm waters under clear skies, leaving the angel on the shore. This represents the time in the man's life when he accepts salvation and can depart from the guidance of others. *Youth* is the only painting in which storm clouds are absent from the sky, symbolizing that this is the time when the man's faith is strongest. In *Manhood,* man and boat have reached rapids on the river and angry clouds loom overhead. Here, the toils of life have begun to take their toll on the man's faith. He is less illuminated in *Manhood* than in any other painting in the series because his faith has begun to waiver, and the dense clouds in the painting symbolize his doubt. However, even in this troubled time he is depicted praying for guidance, and God's promise of salvation still shines brightly on his moral compass, which is pointing him in the proper direction. In *Old Age*, the waters have become tranquil and the man sits in the boat, ready to be guided by the angel into the sky. He is illuminated more than in *Manhood* because he realizes that God has helped him in troubled times, and his moral compass, though badly battered, is still illumined in holy light. The use of light and shadow in *The Voyage of Life* not only implies that the man and the boat are facets of the same entity, but also makes clear the fact that this association is crucial to understanding Cole's allegory of the spiritual guidance of man. However, light and shadow are not the only tools Cole uses to point out this union.

Common aging patterns are utilized extensively in *The Voyage of Life* to further show that man and boat are one. In *Childhood* and *Youth,* the front and sides of the boat are covered in ornate and swirling designs. In *Manhood,* the designs have begun to fade on the sides of the boat and they cover less of the boat then in the previous paintings. In *Old Age,* the ornate designs have all but completely faded, and the figure on the front of the boat is battered and worn beyond recognition. The aging of the boat corresponds directly to the aging of the man. In early life, the man has not encountered struggles that would cause his faith to diminish or his spirit to fade. As time wears on, however, the man encounters things that wear him down just as the decoration on the boat is worn away in the latter two paintings. At the end of life, the man has encountered many things that have reshaped who he is, the way he perceives things, and how he believes. In this way, the boat becomes a pictorial expression of the man's psyche, traveling on a journey from innocence to imperfection, from spotless to blemished. This example illustrates another important point of the text: that the journey through life, though given purpose and made bearable by God, is not without consequence.

LONG 4

Thomas Cole uses one final device in *The Voyage of Life* to demonstrate the unity of the man and the boat: the absence of action on the part of the man. In each of the four paintings, while he is always pictured in the boat, the man is never pictured taking any action to suggest that he is in control of the boat. He is never pictured with oars or any other tool that would aid the propulsion of the boat. In *Youth,* the man has one hand back towards the stern of the boat, which could imply that he is using the rudder, but his hand may also be towards the back of the boat only by virtue of the way he is standing. Assuming that the man is never pictured steering the boat, serious inferences can be drawn. If the man is not in control of the boat, who is? Again, the idea of the boat as an external representation of the man's moral compass comes into play. This shows Cole's belief that man's course through life cannot be altered by physical means. In other words, it is the faith of a man in this life, not his deeds, which determine his course through life, particularly in the most difficult of times. In *Manhood,* the painting with the roughest waters, the man appears to be taking less action over the course of the boat than in any other painting in the series. This observation makes little sense except in the light that the boat is the man's moral compass, and his action, praying, is ensuring God's guidance over his compass. Cole masterfully uses the actions of the man in the boat to cement the idea of their unity and further draw out his point that the journey of life is dependent on heavenly guidance.

Throughout the paintings, the issue of beauty is frequently addressed. Cole's mastery of landscape painting is very apparent in this series, even though the central theme of *The Voyage of Life* addresses religious questions and does not focus on the beauty in nature. However, Cole uses the beauty in nature to make a very important point about life: that life is inherently beautiful. Beauty can be found in aspects of the landscape in each painting. Even in *Manhood,* when the situation of the man is most bleak, a tree in the foreground offers up a wonderful expression of beauty. In *Old Age,* the only painting in which vegetation is not present, Cole represents beauty in the dispersal of storm clouds in favor of clear skies. Cole suggests that humans can seek refuge from the toils of life in the beauty of nature because that beauty reflects the magnificence of God's plan. Were it not for the tree in *Manhood,* would the man have enough faith to petition the skies for guidance over his craft? Were it not for the beautiful vegetation surrounding the man in *Youth,* would he have the courage to leave guidance behind and travel through life on his own? Clearly, Cole is pointing to nature as man's respite and inspiration for faith in this life.

In many ways, Thomas Cole points out a union between the man and the boat in his series of paintings, *The Voyage of Life*. This unity is essential in understanding Cole's main focus for the series. Cole utilizes light, shadow, common aging patterns, and a lack of action on the part of the man to draw out the unity of boat and man and relate it to his overall focus that the journey through life is hard but is aided by God and is, ultimately, beautiful. But what importance could the works of a nineteenth century painter, regardless of their meaning, possibly have for people today? Many people in today's world have lost touch entirely with what Cole was trying to get across in *The Voyage of Life*. They wander through life, complaining about their troubles, without even once stopping to take in the beauty God has left for us in the natural world. *The Voyage of Life* can reawaken lost minds to the beauty of knowing that they are not alone in their voyage. It is for this reason that Thomas Cole's series *The Voyage of Life* is just as important today as it was when it first came to life on the canvas.

Works Cited

Cole, Thomas. *The Voyage of Life*. 1842. National Gallery, Washington DC.
Delafield, Christy. "A biography of a great American landscape painter of the nineteenth century, Thomas Cole, and a discussion of some major themes in his work." *PageWise*. 2002. PageWise, 20 Sep. 2004. <http://njnj.essortment.com/thomascolebiog_rizk.htm>.

The Instructor Responds:

This section of English H1204 combined two themes: Writing through Arts and Aesthetics and Writing through the Environment. The instructions for the analysis paper had been fairly broad: I asked students to "perform a detailed critical analysis of a text or a small body of texts that either 1) take a position on the role, purpose and effects of beauty in nature or 2) that themselves use some version of the 'beautiful' in nature to convey a message or to render an experience." Students were further instructed to use description not for its own sake but to bolster analysis, and to link their analysis closely to specific pieces of evidence (images, assertions, quotes, etc.). Finally, they were to attend to the "so-what" question: to draw conclusions about significance and meaning from the accumulation of evidence in the paper.

Drew's analysis of Thomas Cole's series of four paintings entitled *The Voyage of Life* arises from an original insight about one pattern in the paintings: the symbiosis between the central figure and his vehicle on the waters of life, a small boat. From the start, the paper considers "the big picture" in elucidating the religious implications of the works. Its forthright opening paragraph immediately orients the reader in the paper's quest for meaning and the paintings' quest for religious insight. A strong, clear thesis helps both reader and writer identify a clear path of analysis, which unfolds systematically and coherently in the detailed consideration of each painting. Drew's explication of concrete particulars makes for a highly plausible, convincing analysis and interpretation. All generalizations are in every case illustrated by examples.

Finally, Drew's paper is beautifully written. His sentences, varied in form and structure, suit the sophistication of the ideas they convey. Carefully worked transitions at the beginnings and ends of each paragraph construct a sturdy chain of reasoning leading progressively to some well wrought conclusions about the paintings' complex of meanings.

— Gyorgyi Voros

Synthesis

5.1 ◼ The Synthesis Assignment

◼ ENGL 1105 — Synthesis

2nd Essay in ENGL 1105: Essay #2 in the Composition Sequence

Overall Goal: to learn how to create a new idea by combining the ideas of other writers who have addressed the course theme

General Assignment: Write an essay that explores an idea that you have formed after synthesizing two course texts.

Skills/Criteria: The essay should demonstrate your ability to accomplish the following:

◆ develop a new idea by combining the ideas of others
◆ support your thesis by effectively integrating relevant summaries and quotations into your essay
◆ organize your materials in a focused, cohesive, and logical manner
◆ write according to the accepted academic standards for grammar, mechanics, punctuation, and spelling

5.2 ◼ What Is Synthesis?

As with analysis, when we synthesize materials, we break them down into component parts. With synthesis, however, rather than putting the parts back where they came from, we put them together to form something new. While this definition may make the task seem daunting, synthesis is actually an everyday activity.

If we think about how synthesis has informed our lives, we will discover how a combination of different elements and ideas is inherent in all we do and enjoy. Some of our favorite treats may be examples of synthesis. For example, by combining two foods, chocolate and peanut butter, we get a peanut butter cup. Perhaps the most interesting examples of synthesis, however, involve items that are quite dissimilar, resulting in new and interesting ideas. Take Charles Darwin's theory of evolution, for instance, which is a fusion of two different disciplines, the social and biological sciences. In music, Ray Charles fused gospel and R&B to create soul. Closer to our contemporary lives we can see how Instant Messenger has synthesized various aspects of computer technology to develop a new form of communication. Synthesis is never far from our daily activities.

While we don't expect you to become the next Charles — Ray or Darwin—this assignment will ask you to demonstrate how reading different texts has helped you to develop and hone your own ideas about your course theme. In your synthesis essay, you should come to a position that neither agrees nor disagrees with your sources, but which builds upon the ideas discussed in those texts to put together (synthesize) a new idea.

5.3 ▌ Preparing To Write the Synthesis Essay: Informal Writing Tasks

▪ Informal Writing Task 1: Summarizing Separately

Before putting your texts together, you must thoroughly understand both texts. Begin by writing a one-paragraph summary of each of your source texts.

▪ Informal Writing Task 2: Locating Points of Common Interest, Points of Divergence, and Points Not Covered

Review your summaries and list the general subjects or themes discussed in each of the texts. Make a note of where they overlap. Where, specifically, are the authors addressing the same issues? List these overlapping issues. Note also where the authors differ, where their principles or approaches diverge. Finally, note issues they have not addressed—these areas may well be your opening for new work on the topic.

▪ Informal Writing Task 3: Bringing Your Own Voice into the Conversation

Make each item on the list the heading on a blank piece of paper. Now bring your voice into the conversation. What do you know or believe about these issues based on your life experiences and your reading? Compose informal exploratory paragraphs, or simply freewrite.

▪ Informal Writing Task 4: Drafting a Working Thesis

Re-read the assigned texts and review your notes and exploratory writing. Develop an original thesis that will allow you to draw on the ideas of the source texts while making an original point of your own. Draft a working thesis, using the following questions as prompts:

- ◆ On what points do my texts agree?
- ◆ On what points do they disagree?
- ◆ Where do I stand on these points?
- ◆ What relevant points about this topic do these texts overlook?

Examples: In his essay "Wilderness: The Human Perception versus Reality," Cody Trotter synthesizes the views of Edward Abbey and William Cronon to create an original thesis. You can read the complete essay in section 5.4. Observe that his finished essay offers clues about Cody's writing process—a process very similar to the Informal Writing Tasks outlined above.

Summarizing Separately

To compose his synthesis, Cody first had to understand what each text had to offer. He uses summary effectively in his essay in the following paragraph:

> In his article, Cronon explains that wilderness is a cultural invention. The idea of wilderness immediately conjures thoughts of the frontier and exploration of the unknown. This image made sense in the days of westward expansion, but it is a little out-of-date in today's world. In fact, this idea of wilderness is becoming even more artificial, since people think that wilderness means an uninhabited space, when in fact the original wilderness had an abundance of Native American people and wild animal species that were callously removed to make way for the European settlers' westward expansion. This misconception of wilderness is possibly best shown by the example of Yosemite National Park. Here is a huge expanse of land, a beacon of pristine "wilderness," with a giant fence around it. Even the wild isn't really as wild as we think. This is exactly the kind of thing that Cronon is condemning (2–3).

Locating Points of Common Interest, Points of Divergence, and Points Not Covered

As Cody reviewed his summaries, he could see that the two writers were addressing in different ways the same set of issues:

- ◆ Wilderness as a cultural construct
- ◆ The fallacy of seeing the wilderness as wild, external, and far away

He also noted that experiences like his encounters with wilderness in his own yard and in the urban setting of Richmond were not addressed.

Bringing the Writer's Voice Into the Conversation

Cody created a new space out of these unaddressed topics in the two essays; on the basis of his own life experiences, he synthesized a new claim. Living in the country, where his yard is a "virtual zoo," gave him firsthand experience of the fact that "wilderness" can be just outside one's own doorstep. The baby rabbits he came across in the middle of Richmond while working on a landscaping job confirmed his hunch that people who don't regularly experience the wild just aren't paying attention.

Drafting A Working Thesis

By focusing on "borderlands," those meeting-places between society and wilderness, Cody was able to bring an original emphasis to the revisionist definitions of "wilderness" offered by Edward Abbey and William Cronon.

> Perhaps all those people that Cronon criticizes in his article need to realize that wilderness isn't some far away deserted place, like where Abbey lives, but instead is an integral part of all things that are considered to be nature; one need go no farther than the numerous "borderlands" between society and wilderness to experience it.

Your approach may be slightly different, but the steps to writing a good synthesis will be similar.

- Read carefully and closely.
- Thoroughly understand each author's arguments and point of view.
- Locate points of overlap, connection, or divergence.
- Discover points about the topic that the source texts do not address.
- Bring your own experiences and knowledge into the conversation.
- Find an original emphasis, application, or interpretation that can serve as your thesis.
- Develop the essay as a composer develops a symphony, calling in your texts as instruments to create a harmonious whole.

5.4 ■ Student Example of the Synthesis Essay

Name: Cody Trotter

Hometown: Montpelier, Virginia

Major: Architecture

Last book read for fun: *Friday Night Lights* by H. G. Bissinger

Favorite on-campus spot: War Memorial Hall

Advice for other students in first-year composition class:
Revise your essays several times. Also, realize that it is much harder to support a thesis than to think of one.

What stood out for you about your first English class at Tech?
My high school teacher made college English sound scary and assured me I would fail, but when I got here I was surprised at how hard my professor worked with me to help me produce quality writing.

The student comments on the writing process:

As I was writing, I discovered that using a second source to prove my point turned out to be much easier than I originally thought. However, I did have difficulty providing enough evidence to support my claims.

Cody Trotter and his instructor Lisa Leslie

5

Cody Trotter
Instructor: Lisa Leslie
English 1105 Synthesis
October 26, 2004

Wilderness: The Human Perception versus Reality

When people think of nature, they think of trees and animals. When people think of wilderness, they think of Hollywood images of a deserted island or being stranded in the middle of nowhere with no signs of life anywhere. Many people fear the wild, while others dream about it. But the American perception of wilderness may have been misdirected along the way by too many Hollywood tales. In the *New York Times* article, "The Trouble with Wilderness," William Cronon asserts that wilderness is an artificial construction of the American mind; Edward Abbey's essay "The Serpents of Paradise" can help to explain this concept. Perhaps all those people that Cronon criticizes in his article need to realize that wilderness isn't some far away deserted place, like where Abbey lives, but instead is an integral part of all things that are considered to be nature; one need go no farther than the numerous "borderlands" between society and wilderness to experience it.

In his article, Cronon explains that wilderness is a cultural invention. The idea of wilderness immediately conjures thoughts of the frontier and exploration of the unknown. This image made sense in the days of westward expansion, but it is a little out-of-date in today's world. In fact, this idea of wilderness is becoming even more artificial, since people think that wilderness means an uninhabited space, when in fact the original wilderness had an abundance of Native American people and wild animal species that were callously removed to make way for the European settlers' westward expansion. This misconception of wilderness is possibly best shown by the example of Yosemite National Park. Here is a huge expanse of land, a beacon of pristine "wilderness," with a giant fence around it. Even the wild isn't really as wild as we think. This is exactly the kind of thing that Cronon is condemning (2–3).

The amazing experiences one can have "getting back to nature" are achieved only by a select few. Edward Abbey, a park ranger, writes in his essay "The Serpents of Paradise" about his residence in the Arches National Monument in Utah. He describes the problem of mice living in his trailer, which attract rattlesnakes, and to combat this problem, he captures a gopher

snake to keep the rattlers away. He then describes watching two gopher
snakes in some kind of ritual, concluding that "all living things on earth are
kindred" (Abbey 25). These observations occur basically on his doorstep, but
he is still in the middle of a national park; situations such as Abbey's are
rare. Most people live in suburban or urban areas, and even the people who
live in rural places don't live too far away from highly developed places. This
doesn't mean that the average person cannot have similar experiences or
revelations. They may not be as exciting as Abbey's, but maybe they don't
have to be. Abbey lived in the glorified, Hollywood version of wilderness—
the "middle of nowhere" version—which is the only thing people seem to
consider wilderness. He is lucky, the general public might say; in order to
experience the wild anytime, he only needs to walk out his front door.

    However, the same thing is true for many more people than we might
expect. Wilderness is not some sort of elusive entity that we must tirelessly
pursue to find. It is present all around us. I live out in the country, kind of in
the woods, and my yard is a virtual zoo. There are deer, squirrels, countless
species of birds, local dogs and cats, snakes, and green vegetation that is in
some places too thick to walk through. However, a person doesn't even need
all this to appreciate the wild, which is exactly the point that Cronon makes.
In the middle of New York City, which is one of the most industrialized areas
on the planet, there is a place called Central Park, which has trails for people
to walk or ride bicycles on and also an abundance of wild animals. There are
an infinite number of these examples of "borderlands" where civilization and
wilderness meet, and each of them is a perfect location for humans to interact with nature.

    People also have the wrong idea about how to appreciate wilderness.
Appreciating wilderness doesn't mean living off the land in a cave somewhere, nor does it mean that only rock climbers, adventurers, and park
rangers like Abbey truly connect with nature. These people participate in
activities that lead them to have an intimate relationship with nature, but the
average person doesn't need to put forth nearly as much effort or do something that is inherently dangerous to experience that same relationship in
some way. It could be something that is as simple as what Edward Abbey
says: "Before beginning the morning chores I like to sit on the sill of my
doorway, bare feet planted on the bare ground and a mug of hot coffee in
hand, facing the sunrise" (Abbey 18). He experiences wilderness firsthand
almost every day, and all he does is walk out his door and sit down for a few

5

minutes. We could all do the same, and even if we only see the sun rise through the high-rise buildings of an inner city, we have still made a connection with nature.

Another common misconception that people have deals with where people need to be to interact with nature. A prominent theme in the article by Cronon is that the "tree in the garden" is just as important as the "tree in the wilderness" (3). He's saying that a dogwood that is planted in an island in a parking lot at Wal-Mart isn't any less of a tree than a giant redwood growing in California. It still grows leaves, produces oxygen, and is a haven for birds and insects. People take these parking lot trees for granted; they assume that these trees are not a part of the wilderness because they are beside Wal-Mart. However, if we compare the dogwood to the redwood and disregard that they are different types of trees, there is little difference other than their locations in relation to civilization. Yet for some reason, people assume that trees growing in a retail setting or in the park in the middle of the city do not count as part of nature.

But elements of nature can be found everywhere. This past summer, the company I work for was doing some landscaping for a major company in the middle of the city of Richmond, Virginia. While out there, I happened across several baby rabbits, one of which didn't even have its eyes open yet. Here I was, less than 100 yards from a six-lane road, and a just a stone's throw from an interstate, and I found baby rabbits. If people can't find any examples of the wild around them, the reason could be that they are not paying attention.

People's inattention to details isn't entirely their fault. We live in a world where television and the internet are king. Everywhere we look, there's a new movie about the biggest natural disaster ever or about people getting stranded from a plane crash. We are schooled to think that these things are the true wilderness and to ignore the mosquito that bites us on the arm as a mere pest. As Cronon explains, when people are frequently exposed to something natural, they stop viewing it as wild and start seeing it as a part of civilization (3). This leads to new markets popping up for things like hunting trips in remote places or guided rock climbing expeditions. The American ideal of what is wild has turned untouched parts of nature into playgrounds for the rich.

Nothing about the essential nature of wilderness has changed. It isn't any more or less wild now than it was thousands of years ago. Human perception of it is all that has changed. Cronon believes that wilderness has become a product of civilization, a mere myth that, because it is a myth, is becoming harder and harder to find. Edward Abbey's experiences illustrate the common, Hollywood conception of wilderness; and although these experiences are authentic, Cronon asserts that we don't have to be park rangers to experience wilderness because it does not exist in that Hollywood way. I have had experiences with animals in the middle of the city I work in. People need to stop searching for a remote, unoccupied place that shows no trace of human presence and instead take the time to notice when wilderness is right underneath their noses. There is no need to embark upon a journey of epic proportions to discover wilderness. Just take a look around and appreciate all that is there to be seen.

Works Cited

Abbey, Edward. "The Serpents of Paradise." *Desert Solitaire: A Season in the Wilderness*. New York: Ballantine, 1968.
Cronon, William. "The Trouble with Wilderness." *New York Times Magazine* 13 August 1995. 2-3.

5

The Instructor Responds:

In this section of 1105 our course theme was the environment: more specifically, I asked students to think about how humans perceive the wilderness and nature (these two terms are often used interchangeably but they refer to very different concepts). A key text for the class was Willliam Cronon's *New York Times* article "The Trouble with Wilderness" (a shorter version of the article Jeremy Conrad used in his contextualized analysis paper included in this textbook), in which the author argues that wilderness is "quite profoundly a human creation" — not an easy idea to understand. We compared people's views of nature and the wild in order to understand Cronon's assertion that our ideas about nature are only constructions.

What stood out for me in Cody's synthesis essay was his idea about the "borderlands," which he says is a key location for us to experience nature and understand the reality that it is everywhere, not just fenced off in the national parks or located in the great plains somewhere "out west." Accepting Cronon's argument, Cody thought about Abbey's experiences in nature—which most people would think is the ONLY way to experience nature—and his own experiences in Richmond at a landscaping site and in his own back yard. Then it became like a funnel: pour in these three distinct ideas, and out comes a synthesis: "one need go no farther than the numerous 'borderlands' between society and wilderness to experience it."

Writers often say that no piece of writing is ever finished, but rather it is abandoned. Cody worked hard on this essay both in class and for this textbook. He made many improvements in clarity and re-thinking how Abbey fit into his ideas. I would have liked to see more direct quotations from Cronon, but there is no lack of Cronon's *ideas* in the essay. Had I asked Cody to add some quotations, he would have done so.

After the original thesis caught my eye, I was immediately drawn into the essay by the easy style. Cody had done pretty well on his first essay, but he really seemed to "get" this assignment. He took ownership of the idea of synthesis, combined his three texts—Cronon, Abbey, and his own experiences in nature—in a unique way, and explained his position on the human connection with wilderness in this clearly written essay. This was one of my favorite pieces for the entire semester. Thanks, Cody!

— *Lisa Leslie*

Position

6.1 ▌ The Position Assignment

■ *ENGL 1105 — Position*

3rd Essay in ENGL 1105: Essay #3 in the Composition Sequence

Overall Goal: to learn how to develop a detailed, coherent, well-supported argument using several sources

General Assignment: Use the readings you have done this semester and your own experiences to develop and defend a position on an issue pertinent to the course theme.

Skills/Criteria: The essay should demonstrate your ability to accomplish the following:

- ◆ develop a compelling thesis
- ◆ support and defend that thesis with both textual and experiential evidence
- ◆ organize the material to develop a focused, coherent argument
- ◆ write according to the accepted academic standards for grammar, mechanics, punctuation, and spelling

6.2 ▌ Principles of Argument and Persuasion

The position paper assignment calls on you to employ basic principles of argument and persuasion covered in the *Prentice Hall Reference Guide.*
Before reading further about the specific assignment, review these principles (4a–4e).

6.3 ▌ Understanding the Position Paper Assignment

Throughout the semester, your class has focused on various facets of a central theme, many of which are arguable. Your position paper will offer you the opportunity to present your stance on one of these issues through a well-formed, well-supported argument. Even if you feel that you do not have a strong opinion on the course material in general, go back and consider controversial topics that the class raised as a result of the readings or class

*You don't know me. Maybe you think you do,
but you won't really know me until you have
read me. You can't read me unless I write.
Conversely, I can't really come to know you
well unless I can "hear" or experience your
most carefully expressed thoughts, which most
often come in the form of written statements.
While speaking and physical gestures are
important, powerful forms of communication,
the permanence and intentionality of writing
make us rely on it in important personal and
professional situations. No doubt you have
often heard someone say, "Put it in writing."
This admonition alone reminds us why it is so
important to acquire and continually improve
our writing skills.*

— Benjamin Dixon
Vice President for Multicultural Affairs

6

discussions. What were your reactions when a student or the instructor made a claim in support of his or her opinion? Did you present your view of the other side? Were you thinking about what you would say in rebuttal? Or when reading or researching a topic for one of your assignments or essays, did you find yourself wanting to know more about a subject, or did you disagree with a writer or scholar? These are the seeds of a position paper.

When presenting your position in an academic paper at this level, you are no longer allowed to merely use your personal conviction to support your point of view. It is not enough to say that you believe something; you must explain why you believe it, using credible sources to substantiate your claims. In addition, an effective, persuasive argument acknowledges the other side of the argument, anticipates rebuttals, and shows an understanding of these counterpoints. For this position paper, you will use the texts that you read during the semester to provide proof in support of your opinions and to present a balanced view of the opposition's perspectives.

To help clarify your position, it is helpful to think about *three broad categories of claims:* claims of fact, claims of value, and claims of policy.

- ◆ A claim of fact argues that something *is.* The difference between a claim of fact and an actual fact is that a claim of fact cannot be conclusively proven because we do not have access to all the information we need. Scientific theories ("the universe began with the Big Bang") and statistical statements ("over 60% of incoming Virginia Tech students rate their computer skills as above average") are examples of claims of fact.

- ◆ A claim of value argues in favor of a particular judgment (good/bad; beautiful/ugly; right/wrong). Movie and art reviews ("*Million-Dollar Baby* deserved to win the Academy Award for best picture") and moral arguments ("the death penalty is a fair punishment for convicted murderers") are examples of claims of value.

- ◆ A claim of policy argues that a specific action should be taken. Proposals and newspaper editorials are often claims of policy. Whereas a claim of value judges something, a claim of policy proposes a solution to a problem ("Virginia should place a moratorium on the death penalty").

Proof *versus* Merit: Keep in mind that in your position paper you don't necessarily need to *prove* something. You must, however, demonstrate that your idea has merit.

Example: Let's say you already have in mind a *general claim of policy:*

> Guns should be illegal.

As it stands, this claim isn't specific enough — it needs *backing,* in other words *definition.*

Think about what you mean by "guns." Are you just talking about handguns? What about squirt guns, machine guns, piercing guns, cap guns, rifles, or shotguns? You can see the problem: a little bit of vagueness now has you trying to argue that little kids should be put in prison for carrying Super Soakers. By grouping all guns together, you have set up an impossible argument. You have to revise to create a *more specific claim of policy:*

> Handguns should be illegal.

6

The next problem is the definition of the word "illegal." Do you mean that nobody should be able to have a handgun? What about policemen or soldiers? What about people who only collect firearms but never use them? Try this more *precise claim of policy:*

> **Private citizens should not be allowed to own functional handguns.**

Notice how much more precise this claim is already. The next step is to find ways to support your claim. Remember, you aren't looking to absolutely prove your idea. You just need to demonstrate the value of your position. For this you will need to brainstorm and come up with some *grounds,* in other words *supports:*

- Handguns cause thousands of deaths every year.

- Handgun injuries cost taxpayers millions of dollars in medical bills every year.

- Handguns are ugly.

The next step you need to consider is whether or not your points are *warranted*—whether they are logically connected to evidence or to established principles.

- *Handguns cause thousands of deaths every year.* This point is warranted. Most people generally agree that untimely deaths are a bad thing. This underlying claim of value is your warrant, your connection: since untimely deaths are a bad thing, the causes of those deaths are also bad things, so it makes sense that those causes—handguns—should be illegal.

- *Handgun injuries cost taxpayers millions of dollars in medical bills every year.* This point is also warranted. Given a choice, most people would agree that there are better things than avoidable injuries to spend money on. It is easy to make a claim of value that things that waste money are bad. Again, this claim of value is your connection, or warrant.

- *Handguns are ugly.* This point is not warranted. Yes, handguns are not as pretty as flowers, though weapons collectors might find them aesthetically pleasing. Then again, Doc Martens are ugly too, and our national community does not see fit to ban them—nor a great many other things thought to be ugly, like gas stations, landfills, or strip malls. We can make no claim of value that ugly things are bad—partly because we would find little consensus about what is ugly. Somebody out there surely finds Doc Martens appealing.

Not all warrants, or logical connections, are *claims of value.* However, for this sample argument, commonly established values connect the two *claims of fact* about handgun-caused damage to the main *claim of policy* (thesis) that handguns should be prohibited. Though the *warrant* (untimely deaths are bad) may seem so obvious that you shouldn't need to state it, you should always identify the warrants for your arguments, and if you can't find them, you might want to revise. One of the most common problems in position writing is the failure to recognize faulty warrants. The result will inevitably be a faulty argument.

Having come up with several initial supports, you can now consider your audience and organizational strategy.

6.4 Audience Analysis

Although students are often told to "remember your audience!" the practical reality is that all papers in Freshman Composition are written for the teacher. After all, it is the teacher who will grade the paper. Nevertheless, it can be helpful to imagine another audience for academic writing, especially when writing the position paper. After all, to write a position paper you have to be able to understand other points of view; your task is not simply to amass arguments and evidence but to strategize about how to convince or refute someone who may have a different point of view. Imagined audiences can be quite specific. For example, you could frame the paper as a letter urging your congressional representative to support a federal bill prohibiting private citizens from owning functional handguns. Or you could think of your audience in more general terms, like an editorial writer, who must take into account, for example, that the readership of a certain newspaper is generally conservative.

One of your first tasks will be to see the issue thoroughly and fairly from your audience's point of view. Resist the urge to belittle opposing arguments or dismiss them out of hand. Remember that the people you most need to convince are those who disagree with you, and you aren't going to do that by suggesting that their arguments are worthless. Try to honestly consider what the opposite side might have to say. Chances are they are neither evil nor stupid. They may even share some of your values. In our example, for instance, someone might argue that private ownership of functional handguns should be legal because they *prevent* unnecessary deaths. In both instances, the underlying warrant (in this case, a claim of value) is that untimely deaths are bad. If you can recognize and acknowledge what you and your opposition have in common, you can create a much stronger argument. If you can demonstrate that you have some goals in common, those who initially disagree with you will be more willing to listen.

6.5 ▮ Organizational Strategies

Once you have narrowed down your topic, developed a preliminary thesis statement, generated some potential supports (with warrants you've examined), and have an audience in mind, you can begin thinking about the best, most convincing way to organize your argument. Generally, the introduction will establish the importance of the issue (perhaps with a compelling statistic, detail, or anecdote), provide any necessary background, and then move toward your thesis. Here are some common organizational patterns for the body of the essay:

◆ Explore all the counter-arguments in a single paragraph, then devote the rest of the paper to refuting them and supporting your position.

◆ Devote a paragraph to each counter-argument, deconstructing or refuting each one in turn.

◆ Move from the simplest argument to the most complex, exploring the alternative perspective as you go.

◆ Organize the essay newspaper style, with the most important details first.

◆ Concede the weak points first, then build your argument as you go, ending with the strongest point.

6.6 ▮ Drafting the Position Paper

Now that you've developed a claim, generated several supports, and considered your audience and organizational strategy, you're almost ready to begin drafting. Depending on the particular assignment, before you begin drafting you may have to decide which point of view will work best for your position and audience. Consider the following points:

Do you plan to include your own personal experiences? If so, then perhaps first person point of view is the most appropriate choice for your paper. One advantage of first person is that it gives writing a more personal, conversational feel; however, these same advantages can also be disadvantages. Do you think your audience will be most convinced by pieces of factual evidence collected from your course texts? If so, then perhaps third person point of view would be a better choice.

After completing your first full draft, it will be helpful to review your work by addressing the following questions:

- ◆ Does your paper seem too broad? Have you gone well over the assigned length? If so, narrow your scope; consider eliminating your least-convincing point(s).

- ◆ Does your paper seem shallow? Is it too short? Expand your argument by reviewing the points of the issue on both sides. Have you included all pertinent points and supplied support for all assertions?

- ◆ Did you select compelling examples for support? Did you support all your claims with specific evidence?

6.7 ■ Preparing To Write the Position Paper: Informal Writing Tasks

■ *Informal Writing Task 1: Selecting a Topic*

Here are a few ways to develop an effective topic if one is not specified in the assignment:

- ◆ Make a list of the issues brought up during the semester or related to the course theme.

- ◆ Expand the list if you see subtopics of interest.

- ◆ Eliminate those issues about which you have no opinion.

- ◆ Eliminate any topics if you can't understand and fairly appraise the other side.

- ◆ Select a topic from the list of remaining potential topics. Freewrite for ten minutes about the topic. Re-read your freewrite and underline any preliminary thesis statements you find. Repeat again using another topic from the list. Keep repeating until you have a topic and preliminary thesis statement that you want to refine and further explore. What kind of claim will you be making with your thesis statement?

- ◆ Even if you are not required to clear your topic with your instructor, you might want to discuss it with him or her before writing your first draft.

■ *Informal Writing Task 2: Gathering Evidence*

The strength of your argument depends in large part on the evidence you present. Be sure to choose quality evidence from your course texts (and/or personal experience) to help convince your audience.

6

- Re-read course texts relevant to your position.

- In those course texts, identify (underline or highlight) potential evidence to use in your paper.

- After re-reading and identifying potential evidence, list the most compelling points that *support* your position. Then list some of the most compelling points that *counter* it.

■ *Informal Writing Task 3: Organizing the Position Paper*

- Make a brief outline of your position paper, perhaps using one of the organizational strategies discussed above. You don't need a detailed outline at this stage.

- Consider the effectiveness of the strategy you've chosen in relation to your topic, position, and audience.

- Experiment with your outline. Would your argument be as effective if the order of your main points were rearranged? When should you address counter-arguments?

- When you are satisfied with the order, fill in the outline with the details you plan to use.

6

6.8 Student Examples of the Position Paper

Name: Kevan David Connery

Hometown: Wickford, Rhode Island

Major: Architecture

Last book read for fun: *War and Peace* by Leo Tolstoy

Favorite on-campus spot: The Plaza in front of Cowgill Hall

Advice for other students in first-year composition class:
Write about topics that you truly care about. Also, when the class is having a discussion, it's important to share your views. Hesitating to do so only hinders your development as both a writer and thinker.

What stood out for you about your first English class at Tech?
The most important part of my first English class at Tech was the discussion-based structure of the class.

The student comments on the writing process:

Kevan Connery and his instructor Suzanne Reisinger

I decided to write about the importance of a dramatic increase in recycling in the U.S. simply because it is a problem being ignored today that will haunt future generations. The idea came fairly easily to me because it was a topic about which I feel very passionate. I've always felt that writing with sincerity and conviction produces the best work.

6

Kevan Connery
Instructor: Suzanne Reisinger
English 1105 Position
15 November 2004

The Necessity for Change

Every day people use and dispose of materials in trash bins that could and should have been recycled. Such a trend causes innumerable consequences. It is a pattern sending the planet toward disaster, a widespread problem polluting the world. People simply are not recycling enough. This problem is especially noticeable in the United States where people are not taking the initiative to recycle. The United States government should develop and enforce national legislation that would make it mandatory for individuals to recycle.

Since the American Revolution in the eighteenth century, the American lifestyle has revolved around the concept of freedom. Throughout American history, however, laws have been created and imposed on American citizens for the good of the American people. The time has come to expand this benefit as not only for the good of the American people but also for the good of the American environment. Many activists would argue that such legislation would infringe upon the civil rights of the American people, and they would view mandatory recycling laws as unjust and oppressive. Their opinions are just and rational, yet action must be taken to help restore and revitalize the planet.

According to the Office of Waste Reduction and Recycling at the University of North Carolina at Chapel Hill, although Americans represent only about "five percent of the world's population, they are responsible for over fifty percent of the world's trash, eighty-four percent of which is recyclable" ("Waste Facts"). As the ruling body of a major world power, the United States government is responsible for setting an example for other developing countries to follow. If the American government continues to allow immense amounts of trash to be thrown into landfills, however, the earth's environment could be destroyed forever. As the Office of Waste Reduction and Recycling at UNC notes, a major problem with landfills is that they trap the methane gas produced when biodegradable waste breaks down. When a landfill develops a leak, this methane gas is released into the atmosphere where it becomes a potent greenhouse gas ("Waste Facts"). Landfills also leak other hazardous materials, such as acid from batteries, directly into the environment. These problems suggest that the number of landfills being produced each year in the United States should be drastically reduced. To do this, however, the nation must increase the amount of material it recycles, even if that means by force of law.

As a technologically advanced society, America relies entirely on energy to fuel its vast consumer market. In the last century, however, it has become evident through research conducted by the Energy Information Administration that the United States uses more energy than any other nation. Enforcing mandatory recycling laws will certainly cause the energy the United States consumes to decline. Recent studies have shown that "recycling paper uses 60 percent less energy than manufacturing paper from virgin timber" ("Waste Facts"). Other research proves that recycling aluminum cans requires 95 percent less energy than producing aluminum cans by other means ("Waste Facts"). An increase in recycling in the United States will save energy and will help conserve natural resources such as trees and metals.

In an effort to motivate people to recycle, many grocery stores and state governments in the United States have used the direct compensation technique in which individuals receive cash in exchange for recyclable materials (Energy Information Administration). Although this method has slightly increased recycling across the country, it has not solved the issue that Americans are throwing away substantial amounts of materials that could be recycled and reused. Some cities and states have passed laws and ordinances mandating that citizens recycle at least part of their trash (Energy Information Administration). In such areas, the number of pounds of material recycled each year has doubled (Energy Information Administration), proving that mandatory recycling laws on a national level will drastically increase recycling in the United States.

The United States government needs to devise a system which mandates that every household across the nation recycle a certain percentage of its trash. Such quotas should also be placed upon businesses, public schools, and universities, and the government could then compensate those institutions that reach their quotas and penalize those that do not. Doing so will also require a national collection agency that would monitor and collect the recyclable materials. Although such an effort would require substantial amounts of funding, it would prove to be beneficial to the environment and would also create millions of jobs across the nation.

6

Americans are producing waste in amounts that increase exponentially each year ("Waste Facts"), and this trend produces a guaranteed uncertainty for the future of the planet. The discouraging aspect is not the situation itself, but the fact that few people seem to really care about the environment and its future. In his essay "The Conundrum of Consumption," Alan Thein Durning states that "We [Americans] are responsible for a disproportionate share of all the environmental challenges facing humanity" (373), but this is a fact that most Americans choose to disregard. The time has come for the United States government to correct the situation. For too long the government has left the choice to recycle up to individuals and communities. Laws must be enacted to halt the dangerous amounts of waste that accumulate each year. It is a challenge that demands much work both from the United States government and its citizens, but every effort made will give life back to an already dying planet. Tomorrow will be decided by the actions people take today.

Works Cited

Durning, Alan Thein. "The Conundrum of Consumption." *Literature and the Environment.* Ed. Lorraine Anderson, John P. O'Grady, Scott Slovic. New York: Longman, 1999. 372-376.

Energy Information Administration. Sept. 2000. 6 Nov. 2004 <http://www.eia.doe.govl>.

"Waste Facts." *Office of Waste Reduction and Recycling: University of North Carolina at Chapel Hill.* Sept. 2004. 6 Nov. 2004 <http://www.fac.unc.edu/WasteReduction>.

6

The Instructor Responds:

The course title for Kevan's class was Writing Through the Environment. Readings throughout the semester concerned environmental questions; thus, his topic of mandatory recycling was a particularly pertinent one.

Kevan worked hard to integrate class assignments with his understanding of the course theme. One essay read early in the semester, Alan Thein Durning's "The Conundrum of Consumption," argues that consumption practices in rich nations such as the United States virtually assure the continuation of a substandard level of comfort in less developed nations. With that essay in mind, Kevan turned to questions about practical actions that could be taken to address problems concerning the environment. Following class discussions about the recycling bins supplied to each dorm room on the Virginia Tech campus and the recycling programs in various municipalities around the country, he settled on his topic.

A position paper should fulfill several requirements: first of all, it should posit a clear thesis that is open to debate. That is, the thesis should be a statement with which not everyone will agree. The thesis should be clearly stated. And the paper should offer compelling evidence — not just personal opinion — that supports the thesis.

Kevan's paper does all of the above, and does it effectively.

— Suzanne Reisinger

6

Name: Jenna Glotz

Hometown: Midlothian, Virginia

Major: Marketing/Management

Last book read for fun: *The Da Vinci Code* by Dan Brown

Favorite on-campus spot: Squires Student Center, especially Au Bon Pain

Advice for other students in first-year composition class:
Test your different topic ideas before writing your paper. Prewriting is helpful in order to get your different thoughts written down; then you will see which topic will have the best potential for a good paper. I wish I had taken revising more seriously. It is very important to get more than one person to peer-edit your paper because it is very easy to overlook grammatical errors.

What stood out for you about your first English class at Tech?
I really enjoyed in-class discussions on each short essay we read throughout the semester.

The student comments on the writing process:

Before writing my paper, I picked the essay we read in class on which I had the strongest opinion. I made a list of the topics the author mentioned in the essay and why I opposed them. Then I thought of examples that related to the Virginia Tech campus itself. After writing down my ideas and position on the subject, starting my essay was easy.

Jennifer Barton and her student Jenna Glotz

Jenna Glotz
Instructor: Jennifer Barton
English 1105 Position
15 November 2004

Technology Unites Community

Communication and connection throughout our society are based on one thing: technology. As we grow older, technology is continually changing and prospering. Advances such as the internet help us to sustain a community by allowing us to keep in touch with others, explore new ideas and interests, and keep our society superior in technology. Without the influence of technology on our communities, society would be very different. Technology makes for a fast-paced environment, and newer generations, like the students at Virginia Tech, grow up knowing only the benefits of living with technology. The community of students, faculty, and staff at Virginia Tech would not be strong if it were not for technology. Although in his essay "Pseudocommunities" David Ehrenfeld argues that technology ruins community, technology has helped to build and maintain community on campus at Virginia Tech.

In his article "Pseudocommunities," Ehrenfeld strongly opposes the habitual use of technologically-advanced equipment in everyday life. He believes that through the use of electronics and electronic communication, our communities are being replaced by an unrealistic linking of people that he calls pseudocommunities. Ehrenfeld disapproves of technology and believes it ruins communities; he says, "it seems that almost every advance of our technology brings more social disintegration" (22). In his article he uses examples such as televisions, voicemail, and e-mail to prove his point that electronics are replacing one of the most important factors in our world: community. In these pseudocommunities, he says that "it is becoming harder and harder to maintain the kind of personal boundaries that add strength and diversity to real communities and help them from flying apart" (23). As communities take advantage of new technology, Ehrenfeld believes alienation between neighbors arises and shared experiences diminish. It is clear throughout David Ehrenfeld's article that he feels technology is destroying our communities and weakening the personal interactions between community members.

Although David Ehrenfeld makes a good attempt at backing his point that electronics are destroying our communities, I do not agree with him. Electronic communication is an asset to our lives. Technological advancements work to produce equipment to further benefit all of society in our daily lives. Television helps to spread news, entertainment, and even political issues fast and effectively. Television is a great invention; however Ehrenfeld feels that "the world of television, by inducing passivity and unresponsiveness, has cut many of the human threads and connections that once bound people together into working communities" (21). Perhaps it is true that focusing solely on television does not benefit people's education level and may make them lethargic, but on the other hand, television can bring a community together by televising local events, broadcasting world news locally, and providing topics of conversation between individuals in the community. Students at Virginia Tech unite to support our Hokie sports teams through televised events, and television led to many political discussions between students during the 2004 election process. Without the help of television, we would not be able to keep up with late-breaking news, hear about events happening around the world, or show our school spirit through solidarity and cheering on our sports teams.

Another piece of technology that David Ehrenfeld thinks does not benefit communities is the prerecorded voice assimilation in voice mail. He says, "voice mail is a threat to communities, a precursor of pseudocommunities, in that it accustoms us to dealing with facsimiles of people in our daily lives" (21). The personal touch is slightly lost when you hear a recording on a machine; however, leaving an electronic message does not destroy community. When leaving a voice message on a friend or co-worker's phone, you can record pertinent information he or she can listen to before even calling back. Leaving a voice message on someone's answering machine is kind of like leaving an electronic memo; it allows the caller to leave a brief message and contact information if the call is important. Voice messaging lets people know someone was thinking about them and wanted to contact them, so it is an important function in building community. Without voice mail it would be difficult getting in touch with people around campus. I would have to carry post-it notes around to leave messages for friends, I could not reach the extension I needed at the health center, and contacting professors would be impossible if they were out of their office. The invention of voice messaging has actually improved the way people stay connected within their communities.

6

Finally, although Ehrenfeld thinks that e-mail is a "grave problem" because "it creates the sensation of being part of a community of people working, creating, and playing together for the common good," (22), it is one of the greatest electronic processes invented. Ehrenfeld thinks E-mail gives a false sense of proximity because the person you are writing to may be in a totally different global community, and although this is true, this is why e-mail is so good; it allows different communities to unite. E-mail is also a quick and efficient way to send mail to a person without having to find a post office, put the right number of stamps on the envelope, and wonder if the person ever received the letter you sent. Everyone with a computer and internet connection can be connected to this e-mail system, and unlike the postal mailing system, an e-mail address stays the same even if the user moves from one place to another. The convenience of e-mail may not be the main reason that Virginia Tech requires each student to have a computer on campus, but it is an added benefit to students and teachers on this highly wired campus. Teachers use e-mail to send out important information quickly and answer any questions students may have. In addition, professors use the internet Blackboard site to post assignments, announcements, lecture notes, and grades. Students can register for classes, drop classes, add classes, and view their transcripts at the Virginia Tech on-line website. Even applying for admission to Virginia Tech is done mainly through an on-line application. Without a computer, e-mail, and the internet, it would be very hard to be successful here on campus; these electronic devices help to form a community here at Virginia Tech where students can interact online, class discussions can be held over the internet, and e-mails can connect and transmit information quickly and effectively. Technology has not put a damper on our forms of communication; instead, it makes it easier to communicate and come together.

Virginia Tech, like communities in the rest of society, benefits from technology by using it to stay connected and advanced. On a campus of about 25,000 students it would be impossible to interact smoothly, be linked, and stay organized if technology were not present. Advances in technology that continually update our campus have made the connection between student, professor, and staff closer than ever before. In our current fast-paced, highly developed society it is hard to imagine a world without technology. Although we take for granted how technology affects our everyday lives, our social structure, government, daily activities, and life in general would be entirely different and disorganized without it. From small communities to the larger picture of society, people have become so accustomed to technology in their lives that functioning day-to-day would be impossible without technology.

Work Cited

Ehrenfeld, David. "Pseudocommunities." *Rooted in the Land.* Ed. William Vitek and Wes Jackson. New Haven: Yale UP, 1996. 20-24.

The Instructor Responds:

For her position paper, Jenna chose to specifically counter David Ehrenfeld's argument in his essay "Pseudocommunities." Ehrenfeld's thesis is that new communication technologies give us a false sense of community by creating the illusion that we are connected with other people. When we first discussed this essay in class, Jenna commented on her dissatisfaction with Ehrenfeld's position, and that while she could see some of his points, she remained unconvinced of his thesis. In her position paper, she was able to analyze her reasons for that dissatisfaction and create an argument of her own.

There are a number of things that Jenna does well in this paper: she presents a debatable thesis; she uses a clear organizational strategy; and she cites real-world examples that counter Ehrenfeld's major points, logically leading her reader to her own conclusion. But what makes Jenna's paper particularly good is that she does not easily dismiss Ehrenfeld's points. Instead, she acknowledges what she thinks works in Ehrenfeld's reasoning before respectfully showing its weaknesses and offering an alternative view. This technique allows Jenna to connect with an audience who might be inclined to disagree with her and to demonstrate the analytical reasoning she used to arrive at her conclusion.

—*Jen Barton*

7

Contextualized
Analysis

7.1 ▪ The Contextualized Analysis Assignment

▪ *ENGL 1106/H1204 — Contextualized Analysis*
2nd Essay in 1106/1204: Essay #5 in the Composition Sequence

Overall Goal: to ground a critical analysis in a larger context and set it against the work of other writers

General Assignment: Explore the relationship between a particular text (an extensive set of poems, a full-length novel or drama, or a book-length work of nonfiction) and some aspect of the course theme, using at least one additional text to ground that relationship.

Skills/Criteria: The essay should demonstrate your ability to accomplish the following:

◆ develop and maintain a focused thesis that explains the relationship between the text and a core theme/issue in the course
◆ analyze a text in detail
◆ support that analysis with textual evidence
◆ relate that analysis to a theme/issue/idea outside the text
◆ support that relationship with concrete evidence, including at least one outside text
◆ organize the essay to develop the thesis effectively
◆ write according to the accepted academic standards for grammar, mechanics, punctuation, and spelling

7.2 ▪ Analysis, Context, and Thinking Theoretically

In your Analysis essay(s) earlier in the composition sequence, you broke a text down into its component parts so that you could discover how those parts work together to produce the whole. That stage of analysis is a strong beginning to intellectual inquiry, but there is more to analysis, as you are about to discover. The Contextualized Analysis assignment builds on the analytical processes you have already practiced, but it differs from the previous analytical assignment(s) in that here we are asking you to focus not only on analysis but also on the context of that analysis (and thus on the philosophical implications of analysis itself).

Every act of perception takes place within a context. Every act of analysis is performed within a context. All this is obvious to anyone who thinks about it. Less obvious, perhaps, is the fact that the very context that makes perception and analysis possible also limits and conditions what kinds of perceptions we can have and what kinds of analyses we can perform. This is what philosophers mean when they talk about the *theory-ladenness of observation.* Every perception — and every act of analysis grows out of our perceptions — is thus theoretical. Without knowing it, you have been thinking theoretically from the moment you had your first thought.

The Contextualized Analysis assignment asks you to do what scholars in all fields do: to make this process of thinking theoretically very conscious and deliberate. In essence, we are asking you to read one text (a group of poems, a work of fiction, a drama, a work of nonfiction) through a theoretical *lens* provided by another text. The lens metaphor is particularly useful here, because different kinds of lenses bring different elements of a text into focus — often elements that would otherwise remain invisible.

7.3 ∎ Developing a Compelling Thesis

The best essays usually begin with the familiar and then take us beyond what we can easily see in our familiar territory, far beyond the obvious. However, if you are not able to think theoretically — which is to say, if you are limited to what we sometimes call common sense — you will have a very difficult time moving beyond the obvious and producing a compelling thesis (and a compelling argument to support it). Herein lies the real beauty of theoretical thinking: a well-chosen (or well-crafted) theoretical lens will reveal many non-obvious elements of the text you are analyzing, and it will provide you with a wealth of potential thesis ideas. The acid test of an analytical essay is this: are you indeed showing your readers something they are unlikely to know already? If you apply the theory that you choose in a rigorous, systematic, and creative way, you can't help but show even the most experienced scholarly reader something new.

7.4 ∎ Using Textual Evidence To Support Your Analysis

A compelling thesis is more than half the game. But even if you have a great thesis, you still have to make a convincing argument. In this assignment, that means laying out your theory in a clear, coherent way and then providing a lot of specific evidence from the text you are analyzing.

You don't need to provide an extensive summary of that text; you can assume that your readers have read it, though not necessarily in a thorough, scholarly way. But you do need to provide enough background to allow readers to understand the situations or passages you refer to. Try to do so as economically and as unobtrusively as possible. For example, you don't need to provide an entire family tree or plot summary to explain a relationship; you can fill the reader in with a single phrase the first time you refer to a character: *Amy's nemesis Irving* or *Mama's favorite nephew, Irving*. You don't need to narrate the whole journey to get to your point of interest; you can catch the reader up with an introductory phrase: *transplanted to the Sonoran desert by her father's relentless drive for "a free horizon," Maggie finds . . . .*

As you develop your argument, you will want to integrate as much specific detail as you can, including well-chosen quotations. Beginning writers (even when they have a good thesis) often produce essays that are very thin, more like a sketch or an outline than a fully developed essay. It might help to imagine that you are an attorney trying to make a case to a skeptical and rather stubborn jury. In other words, more evidence is better than less — and the more specific that evidence, the better.

7.5 ■ Integrating Two Kinds of Texts in Your Analysis

The lens text is obviously a crucial element in your contextualized analysis, but a lens is only a tool, and tools don't do any work on their own. A tool is only as valuable as the skill of its handler allows it to be. After you have chosen what you think will be a good lens text, you need to decide (most likely by trial and error) what material to put under your lens (what we might call your theoretical microscope) and how and when to adjust the magnification, so to speak. This process can be complicated, but the success of your essay depends on your making wise choices. If you are writing a relatively short essay, you will obviously have to narrow your focus accordingly, because if you try to analyze too much material, you will end up with a superficial and unsatisfying essay.

Here's an example. You are analyzing a science-fiction novel in which one plot line is about the human/non-human status of a human-created "android." You decide to work with psychologist Abraham Maslow's theoretical hierarchy of needs (even if you're not a pychology major). If you try to apply all levels of that hierarchy to all the androids in the novel, you could spend months on the project and still never get below the surface to the good ideas. However, if you select only the topmost level of need that Maslow claims characterizes the best-developed human personality, and if you select only a few key android characters to determine whether they display that need, you can hardly miss turning up significant detail in a thought-provoking context to power a well-focused argument.

Once you are satisfied with your choice of lens and satisfied that you have narrowed your focus sufficiently, the real fun can begin. You get to demonstrate your originality, your creativity, your insight, and your powers of interpretation. Because the textual elements that your lens brings to light don't have significance in themselves, you must give them significance with your thesis and develop their meaning as you weave text and theory into a coherent argument.

7.6 █ Organizing the Essay Effectively

As you decide on key ideas, you'll want to construct your paragraphs so that they achieve two goals.

1. Let each body paragraph develop an *analytical* point *relating both texts,* expressed (usually) in the opening sentence, *not* for example, like the following, which is simply a plot summary from the main text.

   Plot summary, not analysis:

   > Catherine and Frederic escape to Switzerland.

   Rather, make an *analytical point* like the following *about* the plot detail.

   Analysis:

   > Catherine and Frederic's escape to Switzerland *[detail from the main text]* is a
   > response to the escalating chaos of war *[concept from the lens text].*

2. Arrange your body paragraphs so that they allow your thesis to develop. A static thesis, repeated in exactly the same way, will bore your readers. Allow the wording of your thesis to be progressively more accurate.

Consider the case of this analytical question: Does a history of war (for example, Martin Gilbert's history of World War I) serve usefully as a lens for a novel about war? As you work out what this lens text can offer by way of conceptual aids, you find yourself confronting the classic strategic question any writer must resolve: As my essay unfolds, how do I complicate my thesis in order to maintain the reader's (and my own) interest?

If the thesis simply repeats from one paragraph to the next, your own thinking fails to deepen and your reader's interest, as well as your own interest, burns out quickly. Notice the progression in the following topic sentences from a six-paragraph paper:

> Paragraph 1 (initial, simple version of thesis): In Hemingway's *A Farewell to Arms,* Frederic and Catherine negotiate what historian Martin Gilbert calls "the chaos of war."

> Paragraph 2: During the Italian Retreat in World War I, the novel accurately reflects the chaotic reality of war—physical, emotional, and spiritual—as Gilbert defines it.

> Paragraph 3: In the escape segment, however, Frederic and Catherine marginalize the reality of war by fleeing to Switzerland, where they are affected only by newspaper accounts.

> Paragraph 4: In March 1918, death comes not from war but from the complications of childbirth; Gilbert's frame of history disappears.

> Paragraph 5: At the novel's conclusion, Frederic evades the dislocations of a war-torn economy, to which he will apparently not contribute. Again, he steps out of the frame established by Gilbert, but in making this essentially chaotic move, he validates Gilbert's thesis.

> Paragraph 6 (conclusion, with refined thesis): In *A Farewell to Arms,* Frederic and Catherine negotiate the chaotic realities of war, as Gilbert defines them, by confronting them, rejecting them, and finally evading them.

The progression of these thesis sentences reads like a summary of an essay that begins simply enough. But as a result of patiently working through what the text does, at each step enriched by drawing from both Gilbert's book and key passages from the novel, that initial thesis grows to the more complicated finding in the last paragraph. We have learned from Gilbert how to sharpen our awareness of the realities of war, but we have also worked out the details of just what it means for these protagonists to have *negotiated* those realities through the subtleties of their ideas, actions, and interactions.

7.7 ■ Preparing To Write the Contextualized Analysis Essay: Informal Writing Tasks

■ *Informal Writing Task 1*

Divide a page and write a summary of your lens text in the left-hand column. In the right-hand column, for each point, write what it causes you to see in your main text in a new way or at greater depth.

■ *Informal Writing Task 2*

As for Analysis I and II, develop focusing questions to help you discover and perhaps narrow your topic. For example:

- What surprised you?
- What doesn't seem to fit?
- What details do you notice?
- What confuses you?
- What patterns do you notice?
- What is the overall effect of each text?
- Was either text easy or difficult to read? Why?
- What questions does the main text raise?
- What position does the lens text take on the main text's questions?
- What rhetorical techniques do the texts use?
- What conflicts do you see either between or within the texts?

■ *Informal Writing Task 3*

Develop a working thesis. Most often, the thesis in any analysis essay answers a "how" or "why" question. To get started, you might try to answer questions like these:

- How does the lens text's idea of _____ relate to the main text's _____?
- How does the main text demonstrate _____ from the lens text?
- How does the lens text conflict or agree with your own vision of the main text?
- How does the pattern you found through the lens text contribute to the meaning of the main text?

■ *Informal Writing Task 4*

Develop textual evidence from both texts that supports your answer/thesis.

List pieces of potential evidence that you think might support your thesis, including quotations.

7.8 ■ Student Example of the Contextualized Analysis Essay

Name: Jeremy Conrad

Hometown: Carlisle, Pennsylvania

Major: Political Science

Last book read for fun: *Travels with Charley* by John Steinbeck

Favorite on-campus spot: Lane Stadium

Advice for other students in first-year composition class:
Don't be afraid to develop an individual style. There is no standard paradigm for great writing. English should serve as a tool for improving the way you understand and communicate with the world. People judge you by the words you speak and write.

What stood out for you about your first English class at Tech?
My first English course at Tech taught me to think about writing and analyzing literature in ways I had never before considered. We discussed the role of English in all forms of media.

The student comments on the writing process:

When I wrote this essay, I wanted to choose topics that really interested me. I've always had a fascination with both Lewis & Clark and the space program, and they fit perfectly into my contextualized analysis. One thing I struggled with was the inclusion of textual references. For me, it is always difficult to smoothly transition between quotations and original

Gyorgyi Voros and her student Jeremy Conrad

writing without altering the flow of the piece. This was an area that was greatly improved through the revision process. Reading over and revising my work really helped to make those transitions more seamless.

7

Jeremy Conrad
Instructor: Gyorgyi Voros
English H1204 Contextualized Analysis
October 19, 2004

From Lewis & Clark to Neil Armstrong

In his essay "The Trouble with Wilderness," William Cronon wrote, "No matter what the angle from which we regard it, wilderness offers us the illusion that we can escape the cares and troubles of the world in which our past has ensnared us" (80). The aim of his essay was to explain several ways in which the idea of "wilderness" has become a series of cultural constructions rather than a literal place. One of these cultural constructs revolves around the idea that people have come to view "wilderness" as a place that needs to be explored, colonized, and made to be "American." Another cultural construction of "wilderness" comes from the idea that the untamed frontier is the only place where a "rugged individual" can demonstrate his masculinity and become a hero (78). In his essay, Cronon applied each of these ideas to historical examples here on earth, but it is my contention that these cultural constructs of wilderness can be applied beyond our own planet. As the earth nears a point at which its surface has been almost entirely explored and charted, people are once again searching for a type of nature that is no longer present here: the frontier. Since the middle of the twentieth century, they have found this "final frontier" in space. For Americans, the symbol of space exploration has been the National Air and Space Administration (NASA), created in 1958. Included in NASA's general mission statement are the lines "To explore the Universe and search for life" and "To inspire the next generation of explorers" (www.nasa.gov). Using the U.S. space program as the "main text" (with www.nasa.gov excerpts where necessary) and Cronon's essay "The Trouble with Wilderness" as a lens text, I intend to prove that our ideas concerning space are in fact uniquely human concepts shaped by a desire to spread our influence, inflate our national pride, and create new heroes for society.

Over the next few decades, NASA plans on sending astronauts back to the moon and to Mars. For many people, space exploration holds the same Manifest Destiny-like appeal that the western United States did for settlers in the 1800s. NASA believes it is our mission to travel to other worlds and explore, search for resources, and ultimately set the stage for potential human colonization. The settlers of the west felt it was their mission (their Manifest Destiny) to explore and settle the uncharted areas of the U.S. territories. NASA's own vision statement suggests that today it is our prerogative as Americans "to improve life here, to extend life to there, [and] to find life beyond" (www.nasa.gov). These stated goals perfectly embody Cronon's ideas of the frontier attitude: "Seen as the frontier, [the untamed wilderness] is a savage world at the dawn of civilization, whose transformation represents the very beginning of the national historical epic" (79). For Americans in the late twentieth century and beyond, space has been viewed as the beginning of a more modern national historical epic. During a January, 2004 speech outlining the future of space exploration, President George W. Bush noted that NASA had its roots in the 1803 Lewis & Clark expedition, which explored the unknown frontier. Bush went on to characterize the common goals between the space program and the Lewis & Clark expedition. He said "[Lewis & Clark] made the journey in the spirit of discovery to learn the potential of the vast new territory and to chart the way for others to follow. America has ventured into space for the same reasons" (www.nasa.gov). Bush's speech did a nice job of demonstrating that the same attitudes concerning exploration that existed back then are still important today, including the desire to explore new worlds.

Elsewhere, Cronon described the theory of historian Frederick Jackson Turner: "wild country became a place not just of religious redemption but of national renewal, the quintessential location for experiencing what it meant to be an American" (76). The link between this idea and the space program is obvious. Some would say that nationalism was just an added benefit to the space program. Others might argue that the primary reason for creating the space program in the first place was to promote national pride. In many ways, Americans measured their self-worth as a nation according to their ability to compete with the Soviet Union in the "space race" of the 1960s. Without a doubt President Kennedy considered this competition when he proclaimed that the United States would place a man on the moon by the end of that decade. Whether it was the primary justification, or simply a side effect, nationalism has always been huge element of the space program. During the 2004 speech cited earlier on the future of space exploration, President Bush closed his remarks by stating, "We choose to explore space because doing so improves our lives and lifts our national spirit . . . So let us

7

continue the journey" (www.nasa.gov). Clearly, national pride has served as a major influence on our ideas of wilderness.

In addition to the other influences, scientists are also drawn to space as a final rugged, treacherous place to challenge them. Beyond just exploration and settlement, much of the appeal of space seems to come from the wild and savage danger posed by other planets. Our exploration of space holds striking connections to the frontier/wilderness influences cited by Cronon. He wrote of Americans, "they lamented not just a lost way of life but the passing of the heroic men who had embodied that life" (77). Indeed, the space exploration program has produced some of the most celebrated heroes in the history of this country. So what has led these astronauts to put their lives on the line traveling into the cold vacuum of space? Theodore Roosevelt answered this question over one hundred years ago, although the men he spoke of were only traveling into the backcountry of the United States. He said of this breed of man: "Hard and dangerous though his existence is, it has yet a wild attraction that strongly draws to it his bold, free spirit" (77). Though time has passed and the circumstances are very different, it seems these same attitudes hold true today. Cronon summed up man's attitudes about this subject well: "Seen as the bold landscape of frontier heroism, it [the wild] is the place of youth and childhood, into which men escape by abandoning their pasts and entering a world of freedom where the constraints of civilization fade into memory" (79). Traveling into the perilous depths of space has given the astronauts (modern rugged individualists) a place to be heroic, and Americans have eagerly embraced these heroes. Upon initially visiting the website www.nasa.gov, a visitor is greeted with two videos hosted by Apollo 11 crewmates Neil Armstrong and Buzz Aldrin. These men serve as the public ambassadors of NASA, and this is just one example of how astronauts have been glorified.

Whether conquering the western expanses of the early United States or setting foot on a distant world, humans have always highly valued wilderness experiences. As William Cronon has stated so well, we have always sought wilderness because doing so "reinfused [us] with a vigor, an independence, and a creativity that were the source of American democracy and national character" (76). In short, by pursuing new frontiers of exploration and colonization, we are reminded of the ideals that make America great. Charting new territory has brought us a sense of national pride, allowed us to extend our influence, created generations of heroes, and permitted us to escape from the things we dislike most about civilization.

CONRAD 4

Works Cited

Cronon, William. "The Trouble with Wilderness; or, Getting Back to the Wrong Nature." *Uncommon Ground: Rethinking the Human Place in Nature.* Ed. William Cronon. New York: Norton, 1996. 69–90.
National Aeronautics and Space Administration. Ed. Jim Wilson. 23 October 2004. NASA. 19 October 2004. <http://www.nasa.gov/home/>.

The Instructor Responds:

The instructions for the contextualized analysis paper assigned to this section of English H1204 asked students to "ground a critical analysis in a larger context and set it against the work of other writers." The class had been examining environmental issues in the light of aesthetic considerations. The "lens" text Jeremy Conrad chose, an essay by the environmental historian William Cronon entitled "The Trouble with Wilderness," links the glorification of wilderness with American imperialism, Manifest Destiny, individualism, escapism, and the neglect of utilitarian spaces in favor of "pristine" places. Jeremy's main text was the U.S. space program in general and NASA's mission statement, as it appears on its website, in particular.

Jeremy uses the framework of Cronon's notions of wilderness to characterize the assumptions informing space exploration, to show how the space program is a direct descendant of nineteenth-century frontier exploration, and to draw some conclusions about the cultural significance of the space program to the national psyche. Jeremy's paper demonstrates how extrapolating from source materials can focus an analysis and heighten one's understanding of a new issue. The paper shows the work of a writer who has fully processed and internalized the argument of the source essay and who has gone on to apply it in an original way. Jeremy's selection of quotations to implement his analysis and argument is exemplary, as is his integration of those materials into what is essentially his own inquiry into his *own* subject.

— *Gyorgyi Voros*

7

The Research Paper

8.1 ■ The Research Paper Assignment

■ *ENGL 1106/H1204 — The Research Paper*

3rd Essay in ENGL 1106/H1204: Essay #6 in the
Composition Sequence

Overall goals: to research a topic of your own choosing related to your readings in the
course, to evaluate the fruits of your research, to develop an original thesis based on your
research, and to weave outside sources into your writing to create a focused, coherent,
convincing argument

General Assignment: Write a 2,100-3,000 word (7–10 pages of your own text, exclusive of cover, graphics, extensive block quotations, and Works Cited pages) thesis-driven
research paper developed in response to course readings. Your instructor may require that
at least one course text be part of the subject matter of the paper. At least four (4) outside
sources, in addition to any course text(s) must be used; individual instructors may require
more sources.

Skills/Criteria: The essay should demonstrate your ability to accomplish the following:

- locate and articulate values and assumptions underlying your own opinions and
  those of other writers
- discover patterns of information within and across fields of data
- evaluate the quality of online information
- interpret the meaning(s) of those patterns of information
- argue convincingly for the significance of your interpretation
- propose a writing project
- develop a focused, unified essay
- support every interpretive claim with convincing evidence
- construct coherent paragraphs governed by a main idea
- accurately summarize source material
- locate and correctly cite authoritative sources to support your assertions
- integrate outside material into your writing smoothly and effectively
- use your research to supplement your points

8

◆ write according to the accepted academic standards for grammar, mechanics, punctuation, and spelling: produce, as a capstone to a year's work in composition, a finished formal document that contains on average no more than one grammatical, mechanical, punctuation, or spelling error per 300 words (estimated 300 words per page)

8.2 ▌ Overview

The Research Paper is the capstone assignment for the First-Year Composition Program. It will draw upon everything you have learned and practiced in ENGL 1105/1106/H1204. To write the Research Paper, you will need to go through a number of steps:

◆ generate a topic for research and a research question, based on your class theme and texts

◆ research your topic, using books, articles, and library databases

◆ analyze and interpret your sources

◆ develop a tentative thesis and organizational plan

◆ draft, revise, and edit the research paper

The Research Paper is a thesis-driven paper — that is, it uses a carefully crafted declarative sentence positioned near the end of the introductory paragraph to state an argument or proposition, which the paper then systematically supports with relevant, detailed evidence. This thesis statement should not be merely a statement of purpose, and it should not be framed as a question that the paper will explore.

Unlike a report, which simply organizes information, the Research Paper interprets and assesses information and uses it strategically in the service of an original thesis. Unlike an "I-Search" paper narrating the writer's research journey, the Research Paper sorts, digests, and interprets the results of that journey for readers in support of a clearly articulated argument.

The Research Paper project has four parts:

1. Information Literacy Unit
2. Research Question and Annotated Bibliography
3. Proposal
4. Research Paper

8

8.3 The Information Literacy Unit

There are five components to the Information Literacy Unit, which is designed to prepare you to do college-level research.

1. Locating materials and services in the library

   In this component, students will take a 45-minute tour of the library (on their own time). The library staff offers tours several times a week, mornings, afternoons, and evenings. No pre-registration is required. Tour schedules can be found at http://www.lib.vt.edu/research/instruct/toursked.html. Students will be given a quiz after the tour, which the library staff will grade and return to the instructor.

2. Navigating the library website

3. Searching Addison to find books and journal titles based on found article citations

4. Searching article databases to locate articles on your topic

   These three components will be covered in a classroom session in Newman Library. Your instructor will schedule this session during your regular class time. You will complete in-class worksheets as part of the session.

5. Thinking critically about web pages

   This component will be covered in an online, self-paced tutorial that is available at http://www.lib.vt.edu/research/evaluate/evaluating.html.

After finishing the tutorial, you will complete an online exercise that will be e-mailed to your instructor.

8.4 Developing a Research Question

The first step in the Research Project is coming up with a specific question that will guide your research. The first step in developing a good Research Question is to reflect on the course. What topics discussed in class or in the readings have most interested you? Or perplexed you? Or angered you? Or saddened you? Or inspired you? Questions like these will lead you to the question that will be the basis for your final project in First-Year Composition. The ideal research question is one to which you truly want to know answers. This kind of question will keep you interested and sustain your research. You may have to develop such a question in stages. In fact, you may have to do some research to help you to develop and refine your research question. Different instructors will handle this process in different ways. Some instructors will want you to have a specific research question before you begin consulting sources. Others will prefer that you begin with a more fluid question and move gradually toward a more specific question.

Your instructor will check your research question early in the process and perhaps suggest that you be more specific or more focused. *Your instructor must approve your research question before you can move on to the next stage.*

8.5 Developing a Manageable Topic

Narrowing your topic to make it manageable within the time frame and page constraints of your essay is one of the most difficult parts of this process. One way to narrow a topic that is obviously too broad is to break it down into smaller subtopics, then choose one of these sub-topics. In the "Focusing a Topic/Subject Grid" below, we provide an example of this technique. Some students do a quick search in InfoTrac to see what kinds of articles have been published recently in their subject area to help them narrow their topic.

Focusing a Topic/Subject

Topic	Focus	Narrower Focus	Subject Area	Possible Databases
drugs	1 drug education	1a dangers of addictive drugs	Education	ERIC
		1b peer pressure and drugs	Education Psychology	ERIC PsycInfo
		1c use of prescription drugs	Nursing Medicine	CINAHL Medline
	2 drug abuse	2a economic effects of addicted employees	Business	ABI/INFORM General Business File
		2b physical problems of drug-addicted infants	Medicine	Medline
		2c loss of custody of drug-addicted infants	Sociology	Sociology Abstracts

8.6 ▮ Using Virginia Tech Library Resources To Research Your Topic

These days, research most often begins online. At Virginia Tech, that means going to the University Libraries website at www.lib.vt.edu. Here you can access all of the essential information resources, including Addison (our online catalog), and over 200 databases for finding articles by topic. Information about services, staff, collections, and policies is also available on the library website.

Almost every research project you do at Virginia Tech will require that you consult scholarly sources — books, articles, and websites written or created by professors, scientists, or other researchers who have extensive knowledge about a particular subject.

Depending on your topic, you will want to search for information in one or all of the following information sources:

◆ books

◆ scholarly journal articles

◆ biographical, critical, or other reference databases

By the end of your Research Project, you will:

◆ know your way around the library

◆ be acquainted with the library website

◆ know how to find books via the online catalog, Addison

◆ know how to find articles through indexes/databases such as InfoTrac

◆ know how to evaluate websites

▮ Getting Started on the Research Process

The library website features a "Subjects" section that will help you quickly identify the most appropriate information resources for your topic. Our College Librarians carefully compiled these lists and have included sources like those listed below:

◆ article databases

◆ full-text electronic resources

◆ print materials in our collections

◆ quality sites from the World Wide Web

◆ statistical sources

◆ government resources

◆ related VT resources

8

Best of all, contact information is included on these pages to make it easier for you to ask questions of our subject librarians.

■ *Finding Books*

The University Libraries' online catalog is called Addison, after Virginia Tech's first student, Addison Caldwell. You can access Addison from the Internet via the library website. Using basic search commands and pull-down menus, you can search by author, title, subject, keywords, and call numbers.

Search results in Addison will indicate the availability and location of items matching your search. The key to finding most items is the call number.

The University Libraries use the Library of Congress classification system to organize most books and periodicals (including both current issues of periodicals and the older, bound issues). The classification system is designed to group library materials of similar subjects together and is used by most major library collections.

For items located in Newman, the first letter of the call number will tell you what floor to go to.

> A – E   2nd floor
>
> F – P   3rd floor
>
> Q – S   4th floor
>
> T – Z   5th floor

Other items, such as government documents, juvenile literature, scripts, and oversized books, have special locations noted in Addison.

■ *Browsing Collections by Subject*

It is also possible to browse the collections by subject. First you will need to find the call number area for your topic.

Try searching your topic as a keyword in Addison and look for trends in the call numbers associated with the books listed in your results.

Odds are that once you find that trend, you will be able to browse that call number area for books on your topic.

You can also browse our collections electronically. Select "Call Number" from Addison's "Search Type" menu and enter the general call number for your subject.

■ Finding Articles on Your Research Topic

Periodicals (journals, magazines, and newspapers) are a valuable source for information about current events or recent research in rapidly changing fields. You can find contemporary perspectives on historical events and issues by looking at back issues of periodicals.

Periodicals are also assigned Library of Congress call numbers. The unbound, or current, issues of many periodicals are located on the fourth floor (current issues of other journals are only online). Most older issues of periodicals are bound together in book format. They are shelved in call-number order along with books that have similar call numbers; this collection is called the stacks. Some older issues of periodicals may be placed on microfilm, and issues published before 1980 may be housed in the University Libraries' off-campus storage facility. Periodicals, regardless of format, will keep the same Library of Congress call number. A journal issue may be found in one of four places in Newman Library, depending on its date:

- on microfilm on the first floor
- in a bound volume located in the stacks
- as a current issue located on the fourth floor
- online

For periodicals held in storage, go to the "Services" section of the library website and fill out an online form to borrow the volume you need.

Articles on specific topics *within periodicals* must be located by using periodical indexes and abstracts. Print indexes and abstracts are located in the reference areas on the second floor. You can find many electronic indexes (called databases) on the libraries' website from the "article searching" link under "Online Resources." You may wish to consult a librarian at the Reference Desk on the second floor to determine which index or database is the most appropriate for your research topic.

To search for the printed copy of an article, do a *title* search in Addison using the title of the journal, magazine or newspaper the article appeared in — **NOT** the title of the article itself. Be sure to skip "A," "An," or "The" at the beginning of the title. Searching by journal title will tell you if the University Libraries own the periodical and, if so, where the printed copy is located.

8

■ *Finding Periodicals in Newman Library*

◆ Storage: This off-campus facility contains older/less used materials. These materials must be requested using an online form identified as a "courier request": click "All forms" under "Services" on the library home page.

◆ Stacks: The stacks are shelves that contain the general collection of the library. Most older issues of periodicals are bound together in book format and shelved in *call number* order in the stacks along with books with similar call numbers. *For call number floor locations,* see location charts posted throughout the library.

◆ Current: Current issues of many periodicals are located on the 4th floor near the main elevators.

◆ Microforms: Some periodicals are placed on microfilm and located in the microforms collection on the first floor beyond the circulation desk.

8.7 ■ Evaluating Internet Sources

Search Engine Watch <http://www.searchenginewatch.com> estimates that there are over *two billion* Internet sites and that Internet search engines cover less than one-quarter of them. What percentage do you think will be *quality, useful* information? Remember to distinguish between common web pages and subscription-based sources accessed through the web, like library databases.

A copy of the "Evaluating Web Information Worksheet" is provided below. You can use copies of it to help you decide which online sources can be helpful to you.

8

Evaluating Web Information Worksheet

Title of web page: _____

URL of evaluated page: _____

Research topic: _____

Authority

☐ Is the page signed? Who is the author? _____

☐ Are the author's qualifications available?
List qualifications: _____

☐ Does the author have expertise in this subject?
What is the expertise? _____

☐ Is the author associated with an educational institution or other reputable organization?
What institution? _____

☐ Does the publisher or publication have a reputation for reliability?
Who is the publisher? _____

☐ Is contact information for the author or group available on the site?
Contact information: _____

Coverage

☐ Is the information relevant to your topic?

☐ Do you think it is useful to you? Why?

☐ Does this page have information that is not found elsewhere?
List information: _____

☐ How in-depth is the material?

Objectivity

☐ Does the information show a minimum of bias?

☐ Is the page a presentation of facts and not designed to sway opinion?

☐ Is the page free of advertisements or sponsored links? If there is advertising, could the sponsors affect the content or bias of the page?

Accuracy

☐ Is the information reliable and free of error?

☐ Is there an editor or someone who verifies/checks the information?
Who is the editor/fact checker? _____

☐ Is the page free of spelling mistakes or other obvious problems?

Currency

☐ Is the page dated? What is the date listed? _____

☐ Can you find the date when the page was first written, first placed on the Web, or last updated?

_____

☐ Are the links current and do they point to existing pages?

8

8.8 The Annotated Bibliography

About a month before you turn in your Research Paper, you will turn in an annotated bibliography that summarizes and evaluates 6–8 significant nonfiction sources relevant to your research question. At least four of these sources must have originally been print sources. Your goal here is not to scrutinize your sources in depth, but rather to skim each source carefully to determine its potential usefulness for your project. Your bibliography must follow MLA format.

The annotated bibliography will help you learn to do the following:

♦ locate, select, assess, and begin synthesizing outside sources for your final paper

♦ rethink and perhaps revise your research question

♦ manage your time and keep your project on track

If you do decide to revise your research question, *your instructor must approve the revised question.*

Your annotated bibliography must include the following features:

♦ the citation (using MLA format for entries on a Works Cited page)

♦ a summary of the source's main idea and main supporting ideas

♦ an evaluation of the source's potential value to your research project

♦ an indication of what resource you used to find this particular source

Your bibliography will be evaluated on the following criteria:

♦ the number of sources (six significant sources is the minimum expectation)

♦ the quality of the sources (articles from *The American Journal of Economics* are of higher quality than articles from *Business Week,* for instance)

♦ the quality of your summaries and evaluations

♦ the relevance of the sources to your research question (in general, the more up-to-date the source, the better)

Examine the following two sample entries from an annotated bibliography on the research question "What are the ethical considerations of fetal-tissue research?" What strengths and weaknesses do you see in these entries?

Lawton, Kim A. "Fetal-tissue Transplants Stir Controversy." *Christianity Today* 18 Mar. 1988: 52–53.

Lawton notes that nearly all the tissues used in research have come from elective abortions and that 92% of women having abortions said they would agree to donate their fetal remains to research since it would enable "some good to come out of their decision." She also points out a strange partnership between pro-lifers and feminists: both fear that if abortion becomes the accepted method of getting fetal tissue for research, women may be coerced into having abortions and later into more harmful procedures that would yield other beneficial tissues. Significantly, Lawton writes that if fetal tissue transplants were placed under the Organ Transplant Act, which forbids the sale of certain body parts for transplantation, there would be no potential for women to become commercially exploited "spare parts factories." Despite Lawton's obvious conservative and pro-life stance, this article is valuable for the unusual angles it offers on the issue—no other source so far has mentioned either the pro-lifer/feminist partnership or the Organ Transplant Act. Lawton also includes numerous quotations from fetal tissue transplant opponents without offering any statements from FTT proponents; while her treatment is thus a bit lopsided, I may find some good direct quotations I can use here. Finally, she unfortunately takes an unfair cheap shot at emotional appeal: scientists' desire for "fresh" tissues makes them take tissues from live fetuses, she implies. *InfoTrac Expanded Academic Database ASAP.*

Post, Stephen G. "Fetal Tissue Transplant: The Right to Question Progress." *America* 5 Jan. 1991: 14–16.

Post writes that if medical research becomes dependent on electively aborted fetal tissue, an irreversible economic and institutional bond between abortion centers and biomedical science will have been established. He notes, however, that several people have argued that fetal tissue available from ectopic pregnancies, miscarriages, and stillbirths should be more than sufficient for research needs, but the possible chromosomal abnormalities of such tissues make them second-rate for research. Importantly, he points out that we just do not know what the ultimate impact of FTT on the incidence of elective abortion would be. He ends by questioning whether we the living should improve our quality of life at the expense of the unborn just because we can. The most in-depth and balanced of the many articles Post has published on FTT, this piece avoids finally coming down on one side or the other, but rather presents strong cases for both sides. I think his predictions of widespread civil disobedience or of our transforming FT donation into a civil duty are a bit far-fetched, but intriguing possibilities. This essay does, however, suffer from an unneeded tirade against "secular moral philosophers" as Post tries to cement FTT's status as a religious issue. *Medline.*

8

*Strong writing and communication skills
make a bigger difference in academic and
professional success than most students realize.
Nearly all successful projects at the university
and in the workplace owe their existence to
an effective written or spoken proposal that
initially convinces a particular audience of
the strength and value of certain ideas. For
instance, scientific research attracts enormous
amounts of money and resources, and the
allocation of that funding is based almost exclusively on written
proposals. These proposals must make the case that the work is
valuable, and how well these documents are written is just as
important as their intellectual content.*

—Mark McNamee
University Provost and Vice President for Academic Affairs

8.9 ⬛ The Proposal

Before you begin drafting your Research Paper, you must submit a formal, one-page proposal that details *what* you are writing about, *how* you are going to write about it, and *why* you are writing about it. This proposal will give your instructor an opportunity to help you fine-tune your approach before you begin the actual writing. *Note: Your instructor must approve your proposal before you can proceed to the next stage of the process.* The specific content and organization of the proposal will vary from class to class, but generally speaking, these are the kinds of elements proposals contain:

- statement of purpose, audience, and tentative thesis
- brief summary or abstract of the project
- brief review of the literature
- rationale for the project indicating what is original about your approach
- description of research strategy and timetable for completion

8.10 ■ Drafting the Research Paper

Once your instructor approves your proposal, you can begin drafting your essay. Remember, the research paper is a thesis-driven argument, not simply a presentation of your research. You will want to use your research to support your position. You must select, analyze, summarize, paraphrase, quote, and ultimately weave all the relevant material into a focused, coherent, convincing argument. Make sure that you use signal phrases to indicate where you are using someone else's ideas and where you are returning to your own ideas. Follow MLA format for in-text citations and provide a properly formatted Works Cited page.

Before you begin revising this draft, check your paper against the following six criteria:

- **Thesis.** Does your paper have a clear thesis? Is the thesis specific, well defined, and well-suited to the purpose of your paper? Is it effectively introduced in your introduction?

- **Sources.** Are there at least the minimum number of sources in your paper?

  You need at least four sources, of which two must be originally print sources; your instructor may require more than four.

  Your instructor may also require that one of the course texts be a primary—not "tacked-on"—source in your argument.

- **Summaries/Paraphrases.** Are summaries and paraphrases of your sources correctly formatted? Are they correctly cited?

- **Citations**. Are there textual citations for each of your sources? Is each of your quotations cited correctly in MLA format?

- **Organization.** Are there effective transitions in your essay? Does your paper move logically between topics? Are the paragraphs well developed? Is material from your sources effectively placed in your paper? Does the paper integrate sources smoothly?

- **Voice/Originality.** Are *you* appropriately placed in the paper? Does the essay make an original contribution?

8

8.11 Introductions and Conclusions

Writing guru Richard Lanham advises writers to start fast and "cut to the chase" as quickly as they can. This is excellent advice. Your readers don't want a vague introduction or a long, slow wind-up. They want to know what you have to tell them and why they should be interested. If your topic needs some introduction — some historical background, for example — provide whatever you think is necessary. But state your thesis and get to the argument as quickly as you can. That being said, it *is* a good idea to give your readers a brief overview of your essay. One way to do this is by using the opening paragraph(s) to provide a miniature "map" of the argument to come, one that tells your readers where you are going to take them, what they can expect to see along the way, and why all this is important.

Just as readers don't want to wade though a long, slow introduction, they don't want to wade through a long, slow conclusion either, especially not one in which you simply reiterate what you just told them a page or two before. Rather than using your final paragraph(s) to simply say again what you have already said, use these concluding paragraph(s) to present your now-developed thesis in refreshing terms, to reflect on the implications of your conclusions, to ponder the significance of what you have discovered, to touch on some of the larger questions that your research has raised, or to list some lines of future inquiry. Be careful, however, not to raise new claims that you have not proved — doing so can leave the reader feeling frustrated rather than inspired.

8.12 Proofreading and Editing the Research Paper

One of the most important elements in the writing process comes at the end — proofreading and editing your work. Effective strategies for editing and proofreading papers are outlined in the *Prentice Hall Reference Guide* (sections **2f** and **39a**). Before handing in the final copy of your research paper, review these strategies and use them to give your paper a professional polish.

8

8.13 ▎ Student Examples of the Research Paper

Name: Katherine Beckley

Hometown: Herndon, Virginia

Major: Animal and Poultry Sciences

Last book read for fun: *The Druid of Shannara* by Terry Brooks

Favorite on-campus spot: The Duckpond

Advice for other students in first-year composition class:
Don't wait until the last minute to write your essays. The more time you have to revise, the better the paper will be. Outlines are important. A good outline can be a helpful guide when choosing sources and writing the paper.

What stood out for you about your first English class at Tech?
The essays were structured differently than any I had done before.

The student comments on the writing process:

My first step after choosing my topic for the paper was to search for some general information about wolf reintroduction. Once I knew a little more about the topic, I created an outline and began looking for more specific information. After writing the essay, I read through it, looking for grammatical errors or sentences that needed rewording. I then used comments from my teacher and peer reviewers to do several revisions.

Katie Fallon and
her student Katherine Beckley

8

Katherine Beckley
Instructor: Katie Fallon
English H1204 Research
3 December 2004

The Controversy of
Wolf Reintroduction

Wolves were once one of the most widespread species of mammals in the world. Varieties of wolves roamed across North America, Europe, and Asia ("How the West Was Lost"). In the United States during the mid 1900s, wolves were almost completely wiped out by humans. Now, through reintroduction programs, they are starting to make a comeback. The changes that are emerging in reintroduction areas like Yellowstone National Park show the benefits that wolves can bring to an ecosystem. Wolves rework the food webs of the areas they are reintroduced to and completely change the population levels of many different species, creating a more balanced ecosystem. They also influence the genetics and health of their prey. Despite these benefits, wolves have yet to be reintroduced into many of their former habitats, often because of opposition from people living in a proposed introduction area. Some hunters believe that wolves will drastically reduce game numbers, while others are afraid wolves will kill their hunting dogs. Some people are afraid of the harm wolves will do to themselves or their pets. A third group, farmers, is often afraid of losing livestock to wolves. These fears usually come from information that the media and anti-wolf organizations have misinterpreted or misrepresented. Because the benefits that wolf reintroduction brings to an area far outweigh the problems that wolves cause, people should continue to reintroduce wolves into their former habitats in North America.

Wolves once inhabited much of North America. Experts believe that the population of gray and red wolves once added up to almost 400,000 animals ("State of the Wolf"). The major conflicts between wolves and people started as settlers began moving west. Hunters killed off most of the bison and then began killing other large game such as elk and deer, which were the wolves' main food source. The government had placed no control on hunting, and hunters tended to kill more animals than they should. Some people would even sell the animals they killed in restaurants. Eventually, deer and elk populations grew low enough to be classified as endangered by today's standards. Many hunters viewed wolves as competition for the small numbers of deer and elk remaining and would shoot any they came across. Hunters were not the wolves' only enemy. As deer and elk populations dwindled, more settlers began to raise livestock for a living, providing the hungry wolves with an easy source of food. Average calf crop losses rose to 25%, and farmers decided to do everything possible to eliminate the wolves. Many livestock organizations asked the government for laws that would provide bounties for dead wolves, and several state governments granted this request. Montana is an example of one of these states; in 1883 Montana's government passed a law that set a bounty of $1 for every wolf pelt produced. The next year, 1884, hunters collected a bounty on a total of 5,450 pelts, and the bounty was not eliminated until 1933. People continued to kill wolves until 1973, when the Endangered Species Act was created, which outlawed the killing of endangered species ("How the West Was Lost"). By the time it went into effect there were fewer than 1,000 gray wolves in the lower 48 states, and these were all in northeastern Minnesota. Several wolf recovery programs have now been created, but wolves still occupy only five percent of their original habitat ("State of the Wolf").

Wolves are a major predator and are considered by many to be a key species in the food webs of the areas they inhabit. The effects that they have on other species vary with different locations and ecosystems. Because of its history, Yellowstone National Park is the best example of the effect wolves have on an ecosystem (Gugliotta A8). Wolves were once abundant throughout Yellowstone. In 1914 the U.S. Biological Survey began teaching the military, which was in charge of Yellowstone, how to kill wolves by destroying their dens. The park service, which took over in 1918, continued the campaign for wolf elimination, destroying the last den in 1923 ("How the West Was Lost"). The absence of wolves lasted until 1995, when the U.S. Fish and Wildlife Service released several groups into Yellowstone ("State of the Wolf"). Since then, Yellowstone has become the focus of many studies on the effects wolves have on other species in an ecosystem.

The direct effects that wolves have on their prey, because of the interconnectedness of the food web, have an influence on many different species. In Yellowstone elk make up most of a wolf's diet. The biggest effect wolves have had on elk is a change in the areas in which they spend most of their time. In the absence of wolves, elk were free to graze wherever they wanted without the fear of being attacked. Once wolves returned, elk learned to spend more time in places where there was less of a risk of wolf attacks; this change has benefited several plant species. Elk had killed off many of the cottonwood, willow, and aspen trees that grew in their former grazing areas, but now that wolves have displaced the elk, these trees are becoming more abundant. Willow and aspen trees provide nesting areas for many species of migratory birds and shelter for small mammals, and these animals are prospering under the new forests of trees (Smith, Peterson, and Houston 335–338). The growth of these trees around water has had several more effects on the ecosystem. The trees have reduced soil erosion, improving water quality for aquatic animals. Trees that grow close enough to cast shade on streams cool the water, providing a better environment for fish. Beavers, which like to eat willow trees because of their low branches, have recently reappeared in Yellowstone. The growth of the beaver population results in an increase in the number of dams, which causes portions of streams to become marshy, creating a good environment for creatures like otters, ducks, and muskrats (Gugliotta A8).

     Another species the wolf has had a significant effect on is the coyote. When wolves were eliminated from Yellowstone, the coyote became one of the top predators. As a result, the population of coyotes' prey, mainly young antelope, decreased significantly. Wolves see coyotes as competitors for food and have been responsible for a 50% decrease in the coyote population since their return. Studies have shown that antelope numbers, because of the loss of their main predator, have steadily risen in the past eight years. The decrease in coyotes is likely to affect red foxes as well, though no change has been observed yet. Red foxes are coyotes' main competitors for food, so the decrease in coyotes has increased the amount of food available to foxes (Smith, Peterson, and Houston 335–336).

     The carcass remains that wolves leave after a kill have proven to be of benefit to many species in Yellowstone. Scavengers such as wolverines, eagles, magpies, and ravens rely on carrion as a food source. In the absence of wolves, carrion tends to be scarce at all times except in harsh winters, which increases the frequency of animals dying from starvation. Wolves almost never finish the whole carcass from a kill, so these remains provide a year-round food source for scavengers (Wilmers et al. 913–915). Wolf kills are particularly important to ravens, which often follow the wolves as they hunt. In fact, studies show that an average of 29 ravens can be found at each wolf kill (Smith, Peterson, and Houston 336). Bears, while capable of making their own kills, are another species that uses wolf kills as a food source. Researchers have found that the presence of a reliable food source often increases bear litters. In all, scientists have observed 30 different species of scavengers and 57 species of beetles using carrion from wolf kills as a source of food, proving that wolves are an important factor in the survival rates of many of Yellowstone's species (Wilmers et al. 914–915).

Wolves can change more than the abundance of a species; because of their methods of hunting large animals, they are able to influence the health of their prey. Wolves mostly hunt large herd animals that can be difficult to kill. To avoid injury, they usually go after the animals that are weak and unable to keep up with the herd. The elimination of these weaker animals from the gene pool can cause a population to eventually become better fit for survival. In the absence of a wild predator, a prey species will go through genetic drift, often creating a weaker population (Harper). The genetic change brought about by wolves can also be of benefit to hunters. Whether they are hunting for food or for sport, Hunters prefer not to kill small, weak animals. In an area where wolves are present, the hunters would not be likely to find many weak animals. Hunters are more likely to come across large, healthy animals when wolves are eliminating the weaker ones and causing whole populations to become better adapted for survival.

Though wolves greatly benefit the areas they inhabit, there are still many people who oppose their reintroduction. Elk hunters have expressed concern over the effect wolves will have on the abundance of elk. Many elk hunters see wolves as competition. Some fear that wolves will reduce the elk population enough to make elk difficult to find once hunting season starts. One group, Friends of the Northern Yellowstone Elk Herd, has become convinced that the wolves are significantly decreasing the elk population and has even asked the Montana Department of Fish, Wildlife, and Parks to decrease the number of wolves in Yellowstone ("Wildlife Officials to Closely Watch Elk Count"). Though elk make up 92% of wolf kills, studies have shown that their population numbers have not changed much since the reintroduction of wolves (Smith, Peterson, and Houston 335). Bear hunters have also shown a tendency to oppose wolf reintroduction. Some hunters use dogs to kill bears and are afraid of losing dogs to wolves. These dogs are often expensive, carefully bred, and very well trained, making them difficult and costly to replace, and most compensation programs will not reimburse hunters for the loss of their dogs to wolves. More hunters would be likely to support wolf reintroduction if these programs were willing to add

8

hunting dogs to their list of compensations (Naughton, Grossberg, and Treves 1508–1509).

Another reason for opposition to wolf reintroduction is the fear that wolves will harm humans. For centuries many cultures have portrayed wolves as evil, dangerous creatures ("Fact and Fiction"). An article in an American newspaper from 1921 proclaimed, "The master criminal of the animal world, the Custer Wolf, has at last been killed [. . .] For nine years the Custer Wolf struck terror in the hearts of ranchers. Many credited the story that it was not merely a wolf, but a monstrosity of nature—half wolf and half mountain lion—possessing the cruelty of both and the craftiness of Satan himself" (qtd. in "How the West Was Lost"). Our culture makes it easy for people to imagine wolves as terrifying, bloodthirsty monsters and forget that they are just animals that need to hunt to survive. Today, stories like "Little Red Riding Hood" and "The Three Little Pigs" keep the wolves' bad reputation going. Because of this reputation, some people are afraid of being attacked by wolves. This is a fear that could be lessened through better education ("Fact and Fiction"). Wolves are actually shy animals and tend to avoid humans; there has never been a documented case of a wolf killing a human in the United States ("Too Close for Comfort").

Another fear contributing to opposition to wolf reintroduction is that wolves will kill pets (Naughton, Grossberg, and Treves 1501). This does happen occasionally, but there are ways to prevent it. When people interact with wolves, the likelihood that a wolf will kill a pet becomes higher. Sometimes a person feels sorry for a wolf he or she sees and will put out food or otherwise attempt to befriend the animal. This desensitizes the wolf toward humans and increases the chance that the wolf will get into a conflict with a pet. Some confrontations between wolves and pets can be avoided simply by leaving wolves alone and by not leaving any food outside the house. The best way to keep pets safe is to keep them inside a house or a fenced yard at all times ("Too Close for Comfort").

The largest opposition to wolf reintroduction has most often come from livestock owners. The killing of livestock by wolves is called depredation, and whenever wolves and livestock inhabit the same area, some depredation is bound to occur. Advocates of wolf reintroduction have recognized this as a problem and have set up a fund to compensate any livestock owners who can prove that one of their animals was killed by a wolf. While compensation eases farmers' anger over the losses they have suffered, it does nothing to prevent future depredation. Because of this, there is another way organizations are trying to help livestock owners. A wolf that has been responsible for previous livestock depredations is more likely to kill livestock than one who has never killed livestock before; consequently, wolves that kill livestock are often removed and euthanized (Naughton, Grossberg, and Treves 1501–1509). These methods have kept depredation fairly low. In 2003 the Bailey Wildlife Foundation Wolf Compensation Trust compensated livestock owners for 55 cattle losses, 210 sheep losses, and 15 other livestock losses. This may seem like a large number, but it accounts for all of the livestock in the lower 48 states ("Payments to Ranchers"). On average, farmers in areas containing wolves currently lose less than 1% of their livestock per year due to wolf depredation ("How the West Was Lost").

The balance wolves bring to the ecosystems that they inhabit and the improvements they make on prey genetics are strong arguments for wolf reintroduction. As a top predator, they affect the populations of many other species. The absence of wolves from an ecosystem can throw its food web completely off balance and can even lead to the disappearance of other species from that ecosystem. In spite of this fact, there are several groups of people, including hunters, livestock owners, and pet owners, who oppose wolf reintroduction. The media tends to make the problems caused by wolves seem much worse than they actually are. Statistics show that wolves generally avoid people, pets, and livestock and that they do not cause large drops in game populations. This knowledge, along with compensation funds and the removal of problem wolves, should help more people to accept wolves and support reintroduction programs.

Works Cited

"Fact and Fiction." *The Wolf Education and Research Center.* 5 Dec. 1998.
1 Dec. 2004 <http://www.wolfcenter.org/>
Gugliotta, Guy. "New Predator in Yellowstone Reshapes Park's Entire
Ecosystem." *Washington Post* 26 Jan. 2004: A8.
Harper, Elizabeth. "Wolf Predation on Ungulates." *International Wolf Center.*
1 Dec. 2004
<http://www.wolf.org/wolves/learn/intermed/inter_prey/ungulate_dep.
asp>
"How the West Was Lost." *Sewall Academic Program.* 27 Nov. 2004
<http://www.colorado.edu/Sewall/wolf.htm>

BECKLEY 7

Naughton, Lisa, Rebecca Grossberg, and Adrian Treves. "Paying for Tolerance:
    Rural Citizens' Attitudes toward Wolf Depredation and Compensation."
    Conservation Biology 17 (2003): 1500–1511.
"Payments to Ranchers from the Bailey Wildlife Foundation Wolf
    Compensation Trust." *Defenders.org.* 1 Dec. 2004
        <http://www.defenders.org/wildlife/wolf/wcstats.pdf>
Smith, Douglass W., Rolf O. Peterson, and Douglas B. Houston. "Yellowstone
    After Wolves." *BioScience* 53 (2003): 330–340.
"State of the Wolf." *Defenders of Wildlife.* 2004. 27 Nov. 2004
        <http://www.defenders.org/wildlife/new/stateofthewolf.pdf>
"Too Close for Comfort: the Problem of Habituated Wolves." *International
    Wolf Center.* Sept. 2003. 1 Dec. 2004
        <http://www.wolf.org/wolves/learn/basic/pdf/wh_close_for_comfort
        .pdf>
"Wildlife Officials to Closely Watch Elk Count." *Billings Gazette.* 24 Nov. 1999.
Wilmers, Christopher C., Robert L. Crabtree, Douglas W. Smith, Kerry M.
    Murphy, and Wayne M. Getz. "Trophic Facilitation by Introduced Top
    Predators: Grey Wolf Subsidies to Scavengers in Yellowstone National
    Park." *Journal of Animal Ecology* 72 (2003): 909–916.

8

The Instructor Responds:

Our course theme was Writing Through the Environment, and students were asked to choose a research topic inspired by the book *Desert Solitaire: A Season in the Wilderness* by Edward Abbey. Several times throughout his book Abbey mentions that the ecosystem of the United States is in danger because of a lack of predators. Katherine chose to research this claim and discovered the ongoing controversy of wolf reintroduction.

One of the many strengths of Katherine's essay is organization. In the first paragraph, she introduces the audience to the current state of the problem: by the middle of the last century, wolves were almost completely exterminated in the United States, and the ecosystem has suffered. Reintroduction efforts have been successful in select areas, but proposed widespread reintroduction has been met with opposition. At the end of the first paragraph, she clearly states her argument: "Because the benefits that wolf reintroduction brings to an area far outweigh the problems that wolves cause, people should continue to reintroduce wolves into their former habitats." Each body paragraph that follows develops a main point supported by evidence from a variety of sources. Katherine addresses viewpoints that oppose her own with clarity and courtesy.

Katherine's essay meets and exceeds the criteria for this assignment. Her argument is convincing, well-developed, and well-supported. She has successfully integrated outside material into her own writing. Additionally, her prose is clear, concise, and readable.

—*Katie Fallon*

8

Name: Kim Shea

Hometown: Huntingtown, Maryland

Major: University Studies

Last book read for fun: *The Wedding* by Nicholas Sparks

Favorite on-campus spot: Deet's

Advice for other students in first-year composition class:
Start your essay early! Don't wait until a couple of nights before it is due to get started. It definitely helps to get a head start so you can go back and revise or change something. I now know that starting my essays far in advance definitely helped my grade. I thought that I could get away with putting the same amount of effort into my college essays as I did for my English classes in high school, but that is not the case. I learned that if you want to make the grade, you must be willing to spend a lot of time researching and writing your essays. Revision advice from multiple people helps as well.

What stood out for you about your first English class at Tech?
College English classes were much more in-depth than my high school English classes when it came to the writing process.

The student comments on the writing process:

Victoria LeCorre and her student Kim Shea

I found that the writing process is much easier for me when I am able to write about something I am already interested in. I've always been curious about the war years, particularly World War II. Choosing this topic did not take much effort. Once I had my topic down, I was able to pull many different resources from the library. I flew through my research, mainly because I was fascinated by the information I found and wanted to continue learning new things. I started about a month in advance, which definitely helped in gathering all my research and forming my paper. I had some trouble coming up with a concise thesis. I struggled with some that were just too broad and could not be covered in a 10-page paper. But through revisions with my professor and peers, I was able to narrow it down. Overall, I enjoyed writing this essay and learning so many new things.

Kim Shea
Instructor: Victoria LeCorre
English 1106 Research
April 25, 2004

Sheltered Housewives or
Industrious Females?

December 7, 1941 transformed the American lifestyle drastically. Not only did this entry into war cause significant changes worldwide, but it also altered the status of American women considerably. With exciting, never before attainable, "all-male" job opportunities pouring in, women exchanged their aprons, high-heeled shoes, and dresses for helmets, steel-toed boots, and overalls *(A String of Pearls)*. They quickly altered their roles as mothers and wives to embark on a new journey as unique "pioneers," women in what were typically male industries. Although these types of jobs generally only lasted for the duration of the war, the women's capabilities extracted them from invisibility and opened up a plethora of new and captivating opportunities in the workforce.

Recovering from an economic depression, American life slowly reverted to "normalcy" by the late 1930s. Emphasis was placed on family life; the males' responsibility was preserving the economic stability of the family, whereas the females' task was assuring the material and psychological maintenance of the family (Hartmann 16). This image of women being the homemakers was thought of as natural. Hartmann states that "The majority of adult women experienced the Depression as wives rather than as paid workers;" those who did choose to work were viewed as greedy and selfish, taking jobs away from male breadwinners (16–17). Women thus had very little choice other than to assume their preconceived role in American life. Propaganda and advertisements reinforced a "Mom knows best" approach to many things (Barnard 189). Hobbies and radio shows such as Roosevelt's "Fireside Chats" instilled the notion of families gathering together, participating in activities that were entertaining and stabilizing after years of dismal times *(American Cultural History)*. Women were to rebuild family life and stay home.

In 1939, war broke out among European nations, and the effects of this war appeared in the United States. America aided certain countries to resist Adolph Hitler and his regime. By 1940, Congress, sensing a threat of impending war for this nation as well, passed the Selective Training and Service Act, which drafted men into the military, and the Lend-Lease Act, authorizing food and weapons to be sent to England (Colman 5). America seemed poised to enter the Second World War.

With the attack on Pearl Harbor in 1941, Japan brought world turmoil to American soil. Americans would see great changes to their newly stabilized lives, what Colman calls "the rapidly approaching exit of life-as-usual" (8). Everyday items, such as sugar and coffee, were in short supply, so citizens began to save and salvage. The United States' access to rubber was cut off, and gas was hard to come by. Rationing was created to prevent prices from skyrocketing, so American families planted victory gardens to help feed their country (Colman 8–10, 12, 13). They did not seem to mind adjusting their lives; patriotism swept the country. Newsreels, magazines, posters, ads, and newspapers kept the conflict vivid in everyone's minds. A common saying of that time was "Don't you know there's a war on?" (Colman 14). The country did indeed know and was answering the call.

One further issue required addressing: the men who ran this country were now fighting in a distant war, which meant that soon enough women would answer their own call to duty. Women applied by the thousands for employment. But viewed as mothers and wives and nothing more, they were not freely welcomed into the workforce (Colman 24). Some bosses favored men exempt from the draft, those suffering from disabilities, or prisoners over women. Husbands even went so far as to forbid their wives from joining the workplace. One such husband hid his wife's welder's apron and boots so that she could not report to work (Frank 66). But as the need for workers increased, employers were forced to consider that women could quite possibly perform jobs accurately and with skill. Soon enough, they filled factories, shipyards, and even the military. Against all odds, women had integrated the labor force at last, becoming "pioneers in the American workplace" (Colman 82). These "industrial pioneers" learned how to weld and operate heavy machinery. Some acquired engineering skills and others became proficient in plowing fields at rapid rates. The so-called "housewives" of the 1930s were hired in an array of thrilling as well as arduous jobs. Granted, a multitude of wives and mothers felt as if working were just too dirty or difficult for them, thus preserving the image of women as neat and tidy homemakers, but ultimately eighteen million women gladly accepted their new roles in World War II America (Frank, Ziebarth, and Field 16).

8

SHEA 3

Women trained in various ways. Initially, some were forced to educate themselves by watching and studying on the job. But eventually training programs developed, even in high school courses, when the demand for more women workers escalated. Despite minimal teaching and preparation, females demonstrated their talents, showing the country that they, too, could handle male professions without adversity. These wartime experiences shed light on the ingenuity of women.

While on their quest for equality and visibility, women faced discrimination and sexual harassment on the job. When women first arrived, they had no restrooms of their own, received no breaks during their long shifts, and were provided no lunchrooms in which to enjoy their food. But as they became more common in the labor force, these privileges were accorded. Women also dealt with whistles, cat calls, and name calling by male fellow employees. Although the majority of the time they kept quiet, a few boisterous women would stand up against this rudeness. Oftentimes, men would ruin women's production on purpose out of resentment. They would then lounge around, hardly exerting themselves, while the women diligently completed their tasks without a word of protest. Men also used the threat of causing women to lose their job as bait for sexual favors. Colman describes one such experience: "When another woman, a welder in a shipyard, refused her male boss's sexual advances, he put her out in the rain to work" (87). Ordeals such as these brought women out of their reserved demeanor and gave them a voice that had been silent for years. Their ability to function in such situations exemplified their strength and endurance.

Women also had to cope with hazardous working conditions, an aspect of female labor that was kept quiet. The media and news never included details on that part of the women's experience in the workplace. A machinist from Massachusetts, Althea Bates Gladish, illuminated these alarming occurrences: "There were many hazards in those machine shops. Once a girl caught her hair in the burring machine one night and almost lost her scalp. They shut the machine off [. . .] You had to have your mind on what you were doing every second or some tragedy would occur" (Wise and Wise 64). A phenomenal number of wartime industrial deaths occurred, more than combat deaths before D-Day in 1944 (Frank, Ziebarth, and Field 63). The men of America were dying for the sake of their country as were the women on the home front, though they did not receive well-deserved recognition.

As time passed and the number of female workers increased, attitudes

8

of women began to change significantly. The idea of working as just doing their part in the war effort or helping to bring their men home more quickly was replaced with the notion of work being their new found role. A life of staying at home and raising the children no longer seemed enticing to this "new" woman created during World War II (*The Life and Times of Rosie the Riveter*). Edith Speert, a working wife during the war, wrote in one of her many letters to her husband overseas, "Sweetie, I want to make sure I make myself clear about how I've changed [. . .] you are not married to a girl that's interested solely in a home—I shall definitely have to work all my life—I get emotional satisfaction out of working " (May 154). Feelings such as these were common. A survey taken in 1944 showed that half of the former home-makers wanted to continue working, and 75% of all female workers wanted to keep their new roles as ambitious workers (Gluck 16). They no longer desired typical "female" jobs. They had not only proven that they could handle a man's job, but craved the opportunity to continue doing so.

On September 2, 1945, America's part in the war officially ended. With this change, the employment for women also came to an abrupt halt. An electrical helper at the Navy Yard protested, stating, "I like my work so much that they'll have to fire me before I leave," which is exactly what began to happen (Colman 93). The documentary *A String of Pearls* reveals that an estimated two million women were laid off for no apparent reason. Historians Nancy Baker Wise and Christy Wise describe this injustice: "the veterans' return entailed wrenching change forcing them angrily back to 'women's work' [. . .]; they had proven they could do the work and were frustrated not to be allowed to continue" (4). The old lifestyle of America was being ushered back in with force. It was as if four years of women's hard-earned accomplishments in the labor force would now be ignored. Yet women were not ready nor did they want to return to their old lives.

The years after the war once again concentrated on family life, with marriages and births increasing at unheard of rates. It seemed as if citizens wanted to revert to the lives they had led before the conflict began. Former female war workers once more assumed their homemaking responsibilities, though not for long. Rose Coffield Swanson, a machinist for the duration, explained her life after the war: "I settled down with my family like most of the women did, but I was aware that I could earn money and wanted to. After the kids got a little bigger, I phoned the machinist's union" (Wise and Wise 181). Wives learned how to juggle their family life and preserve a place in the labor force. In 1947, figures of women working began to rise once again. By the end of the 1940s, the number of women employed was higher than the wartime peak (Hartmann 24). With females in such a wide array of industries, there was an employment gain in every occupational field except for domestic service (Hartmann 21). The momentum from the war years continued, encouraging women to progress past the image they had been assigned for so long.

World War II was an event that changed the world and America. The most profound impact of this great conflict is still being felt today. Possibilities arrived that were completely unfamiliar to the housewives of America. Working brought a sense of independence and a feeling of accomplishment to their protected lives. They proved they could handle the strenuous work that males had been doing for centuries. Working in different industries showed women that they were capable of much more than they had thought. Jobs during the war prepared women for future careers that they would eventually establish and affirmed their aspirations of leaving the home to start them. Women overcame many obstacles to earn a place among male workers. These particular pioneers began a radical change in the role of women in American life. Gluck stated it best when she said that these wartime experiences "laid the groundwork for the transformation of [. . .] a woman who timidly defined herself as 'just a mother of four' to a self-confident participant in the wider world" (265). Women are now a regular component of the American workforce, with 57.3% of women working outside the home compared to 37% in 1950 (Wise and Wise 4). World War II gave women a chance to grow and emerge from invisibility, enlarging their status forever.

Works Cited

American Cultural History. Ed. Bettye Sutton. May 2004. Kingwood College. 27 April 2004 < http://kclibrary.nhmccd.edu/decade30.html>.

Barnard, Rita. *The Great Depression and the Culture of Abundance: Kenneth Fearing, Nathanael West, and Mass Culture in the 1930's.* New York: Cambridge UP, 1995.

Colman, Penny. *Rosie the Riveter: Women Working on the Home Front in World War II.* New York: Crown, 1995.

Frank, Miriam, Marilyn Ziebarth, and Connie Field. *The Life and Times of Rosie the Riveter: The Story of Three Million Working Women During World War II.* Emeryville, CA: Clarity Educational Productions, 1982.

Gluck, Sherna Berger. *Rosie the Riveter Revisited: Women, the War, and Social Change.* Boston: Twayne, 1987.

8

SHEA 6

Hartmann, Susan M. *The Home Front and Beyond: American Women in the 1940s.* Boston: Twayne, 1982.

The Life and Times of Rosie the Riveter. Dir. Connie Fields. Direct Cinema Ltd. 1987.

May, Elaine Tyler. "Ambivalent Dreams: Women and the Home after World War II." *Journal of Women's History* 13 (2001): 151–52.

A String of Pearls. Dir. Anthony Ross Potter. PBS. 1990.

Wise, Nancy Baker and Christy Wise. *A Mouthful of Rivets: Women at Work in World War II.* San Francisco: Jossey-Bass, 1994.

The Instructor Responds:

Throughout the semester our class explored the visibility/invisibility dichotomy as a subtheme of cross-cultural contact. By reading the novel that inspired this theme, *Invisible Man* by Ralph Ellison, we discovered the effects of racial discrimination in America during the 1930s. Students were subsequently asked to choose a topic of research that would enlighten other instances of prejudice. Kim decided to explore the recruitment of women into the workforce as a consequence of World War II and curiously discovered the resulting empowerment of females.

Although it is difficult to prioritize the qualities to highlight, Kim's paper deserves high praise. First of all, she consulted numerous, recent, and credible sources which she then integrated with seeming ease into a clear narrative. This clarity issued from her construction of paragraphs organized around topic sentences that introduced and concluding sentences that clinched her arguments. The evidence that she incorporated, including appropriate and interesting quotations, was well-chosen. She also selected precise, sophisticated verbs. And finally, she proofread with extreme care, applying the MLA style precisely. Above all, she created a highly readable paper. Congratulations, Kim!

—Victoria LeCorre

Spoken Composition

9.1 ■ The Spoken Composition Assignment

■ *ENGL 1105 and 1106/1204 — Spoken Composition Presentations*

1st and 2nd Presentations in All First-Year Composition Courses

Overall Goals: to meet the National Communication Association Standards for effective spoken discourse for college sophomores, including the ability to determine the purpose of spoken discourse; to choose a topic and restrict it according to the purpose and the audience; and to fulfill the purpose of spoken discourse by formulating a thesis statement, providing adequate support, and organizing your material effectively and clearly

General Assignment: Participate in two spoken composition presentations in each course:

◆ one group presentation, with 4 – 6 students speaking for a total of 12 – 15 minutes

◆ one individual presentation of 5 minutes

9.2 ■ Introduction to Spoken Composition

According to Virginia Tech alumni, there are two kinds of speaking abilities in which college students need far more instruction and practice. The first of these skills is the ability to listen carefully to an ongoing conversation and respond and contribute in a cogent, meaningful, and appropriate way. This particular ability has long been fostered in the typical first-year composition classroom, of course, through class discussion as a teaching method, small group work, conference teaching, and the like. The second of these skills, however — the ability to make a spoken presentation, to deliver content to an audience in a one-way flow of information from speaker to hearers — is no longer typically associated with writing courses but with public speaking courses.

This separation of spoken and written composition into separate courses of study is a fairly recent development. For nearly 2,500 years, from the 5th century B.C.E. in Athens through the nineteenth century in America, spoken and written composition were taught side by side, synergistically, as students studied the art of rhetoric. But as S. Michael Halloran argues in *A Short History of Writing Instruction* (ed. James J. Murphy, Davis, CA: Hermagoras Press, 1990), a variety of cultural forces — literary, educational, political, economic, and

9

technological—converged in the nineteeenth century to transform the undergraduate course in neoclassical rhetoric into "English composition." The resulting rift between instruction in spoken and written composition in American higher education widened quickly, and in the twentieth century, speaking and writing instruction became distinctly separate disciplines: generally speaking, Communication Studies departments taught public speaking courses, while English departments taught writing courses.

But that gap has begun to close—and rapidly, too. University administrators across the country have come to understand that good speaking skills, like good writing abilities, are *everybody's* business and cannot be relegated to any one department, faculty, or course. Here at Virginia Tech, we are working hard to address the long-standing criticism of our graduates: that while they are very smart people and experts in their technical knowledge, they have not been strong communicators. Every program of study in every major must now work to ensure that its graduates are effective written, spoken, and visual communicators.

9.3 ▌ Strategies for Working Successfully in a Group

- ◆ **Elect a communication leader:** Working in a group means that each individual member is working toward the greater good of the group. There are many ways to make a group work successfully. Take time to get to know each other. Then elect a communication leader. This person will be in charge of sending out e-mails to the group and coordinating meetings.

- ◆ **Work for a single, unified presentation:** A successful group presentation will be smooth and coherent. It is easy to spot a presentation by a group whose members have not worked well together: speakers repeat each other's information, offer conflicting ideas and data, and develop the thesis poorly. To do good work together, do not simply meet once and delegate each person to create an individual mini-presentation. Rather, meet often and strive for unity and consistency between speakers.

- ◆ **Work through each member's strengths:** To begin creating an effective group presentation, you should ask members to identify their own experiences, strengths, weaknesses, and concerns as presenters. Then work with each person's strengths; for example, have a dynamic speaker present your introduction or conclusion, and have a nervous speaker present in the middle. While each member needs to speak and contribute equally, respecting each student's preferences will help you work as a whole and create a successful presentation.

9

*What we hear most from employers
is the importance of being able to write and
speak effectively. Your ideas and proposals
may be wonderful, but if you can't
communicate, you're just blowing smoke.*

—Richard G. Oderwald,
Associate Dean for
Undergraduate Programs,
College of Natural Resources

◆ **Make the most of planning meetings:** Make sure you meet with your entire group several times before your presentation. Before the meeting ends, make sure everyone knows the next steps to be taken. When you meet again, make sure that you have completed your tasks. Always come to the group prepared.

◆ **Practice together:** Practicing as a group is also very important. Make sure your group gets together and practices the presentation out loud a few times before the day of the presentation. As you practice together, listen for repeated facts and unclear transitions. Time yourselves and make sure you do not go over the allowed time.

9.4 Preparing for Your Spoken Presentation

■ *The Topic*

If your instructor has not given you a specific topic, remember that preparing a spoken composition is a lot like preparing any composition. Review the relevant texts. What did you find interesting? What parts would you or your classmates want to learn more about? How have your readings influenced your perception of the course theme? How have your perceptions of the course theme changed? What have you learned? What puzzled you? Freewriting on any of these questions may help you discover what you would like to speak about.

9

If your instructor has given you a specific topic, find a way to make it your own. What part of the topic interests you most? What might other students most want or need to know about the topic? If you were in the audience, what would make the topic most interesting or helpful? What would make you want to listen? What would make you want to learn? Again, freewriting on these questions may be beneficial.

■ *Research*

As you begin your research, you may find that your topic is too broad or that you are overloaded with information. Remember the time limit for the presentation, and make sure you do not try to cram in too much information. Narrow your focus. For example, if you decide to speak about Appalachian coal mines, you might consider narrowing the topic and focusing on a significant historical event.

■ *Avoiding Plagiarism*

As explained in Chapter 3, plagiarism is the presenting of someone else's work as your own. It is a serious academic offense. Plagiarism comes in many forms, and learning what those are can help you avoid it. You must be careful to avoid plagiarism in all of your work, including spoken presentation.

If your presentation requires research, remember to keep track of all of your sources. Refer to your *Prentice Hall Reference Guide* to make sure you collect all the appropriate source information.

Your instructor may require you to turn in a Works Cited page with your presentation. Refer to your *Prentice Hall Reference Guide* and follow MLA standards for creating a Works Cited page. Even if your instructor does not require a formal Works Cited page, it is important that you keep track of your sources in case someone has a question or concern about your facts.

While giving the presentation, you must credit your sources. Be sure to find out how your instructor wants you to credit sources, as particular assignments may require specific ways of acknowledging sources.

Use of exact quotations: If you are presenting an exact quotation, give the source's name and affiliation and then say "quote" and "end quote" before and after the quoted material. For example,

9

> Sarah Marshal from the *Chicago News Tribune* notes QUOTE "Women in the work place are finding new ways to break through the dreaded glass ceiling." END QUOTE.

Use of paraphrases: If you are paraphrasing a source, you still need to credit your source. For example,

> According to John Walsh, a journalist for the *New York Times,* genetic enhancement will change the face of our future.

■ *Analyzing Purpose & Audience*

Beyond the Composition Classroom: When giving a presentation to your employer or to your community, you will always have to consider your purpose and your audience. Your rhetorical strategies will depend on what you want to accomplish and what your audience needs.

For example, imagine you are preparing a presentation on the rising crime problem in your neighborhood.

◆ **To analyze your purpose,** first you need to decide whether you want to persuade, inform, entertain, or motivate. You might ask questions like these: What outcome do you want from your presentation? Do you want the audience to be more informed, write a letter, join your group, believe that your new plan to fight crime will work? If your goal is simply to raise awareness, then you'll need to concentrate on presenting compelling evidence. If you want them to write letters to the city council, your strategy should include evidence that letter-writing campaigns are an effective strategy, along with specific addresses.

◆ **To analyze your audience,** ask yourself the following questions: How much do other community members know about this problem? How does the problem affect them? What abilities do they have, individually or together, to change the situation? If you are speaking in a historically active community, you won't need to convince them that they can make a difference. However, if your community has never gotten together to take on the power structures, then you will need to start by showing that group action can be effective.

In the Composition Classroom: It may be less clear to you that you need to consider your purpose and audience in preparing your presentations for your composition class, since your purpose is to fulfill the assignment, of course. But you need to go beyond that

9

generic purpose and develop goals of your own. Unless you know what outcome you want for the audience, you cannot plan your presentation.

You will be speaking to your fellow classmates and your instructor — at first glance a homogenous audience. Remember, however, that even your classmates are a diverse group of people. Each student has a different background, religious affiliation, political viewpoint, educational history, and understanding of the topic. For any audience, you must ask yourself how you can address their backgrounds and meet their needs.

For example, imagine that you are a computer science major, and you are giving a presentation to your first-year composition class on internet security.

◆ **To analyze your purpose,** ask yourself what you want to do. Do you want to scare your audience into updating their virus protection more often? Do you want to convince them to take the trouble to become even more knowledgeable? Do you want them to join you in a petition to get Virginia Tech to provide a particular security service? Or do you want simply to explain the security issues upon which some plot twist in a novel depends? You would develop a different strategy for each of these purposes.

◆ **To analyze your audience,** you should remember that your classmates do not have your background. You can assume that they know their way around a computer; however, you must remember to limit your use of technical jargon and make sure to explain concepts in everyday language, since some will know only enough about a computer to read e-mail, surf the internet, and type their papers. Any audience will respect expertise, but no audience will be able to act on terminology they don't understand.

These examples of audience and purpose considerations can help you think about your own plans for your presentations. The principles apply to any situation.

■ *Organization*

Remember that a spoken presentation follows the same principles as a written composition. Try creating an outline to make sure that your material is organized logically. Consider the same elements that you would work on if you were organizing ideas in a written composition. Here are some questions to consider.

◆ Do you have a clear and focused point? Are you prepared to make the focus clear to the audience toward the beginning of the presentation?

9

◆ Do you plan to begin in a way that can generate interest by using wit, humor, anecdote, or surprise?

◆ Do your ideas flow logically? Are your points well supported?

◆ Does your planned conclusion bring your ideas together clearly?

■ *Practice*

Practicing is the single best way to prepare for and improve your presentation. Here are a few strategies.

◆ **DON'T MEMORIZE** the presentation! A memorized presentation rarely seems natural to an audience.

◆ **DON'T READ** the presentation! It is very difficult to keep the audience engaged when reading long passages out loud.

◆ Practice by yourself, addressing and observing yourself in a mirror.

◆ Try to use conversational language. Each time you practice, use your outline to prompt you, but improvise the words.

◆ Practice handling your notes or outline — figure out the best way to hold cards or papers, how to advance through the cards or turn the pages, and how to make your notes really useful to you. Make sure the notes are printed in a size that you can read at a glance at arm's length — you don't want to have to hold the notes up in front of your face to read them. If you plan to dim the lights for a PowerPoint presentation, make sure that you can still read your notes. Make sure that you know how to finish a thought that is noted on a card.

◆ Practice looking up and away from cards or outlines. Watch the mirror and make sure you are making eye contact.

◆ Experiment with different tones of voice for different parts of the presentation.

◆ Try to incorporate helpful hand gestures and then repeat them as you continue to practice. Some of the most effective gestures are the simplest. For example, count off points on your fingers. This simple technique helps the audience hold a multi-point argument in mind.

9.5 ■ Visual Aids

Visual aids can be a vital part of a presentation. Visual aids enhance your presentation for the audience by providing additional information, by creating variety, and by encouraging a higher level of audience participation and interaction.

9

Visual aids can help you, the speaker, as well. They can not only help you focus; they can also provide prompts as you present — an often-helpful tool when nerves are running high.

However, use caution when you are choosing and preparing visual aids. If poorly chosen, visual aids can quickly become an unwanted distraction. By considering all of the conditions surrounding your spoken composition, you can successfully choose, create, and execute visual aids that will show you as a well-prepared and confident presenter. Here are some guidelines to consider.

◆ Consider your presentation topic. Be creative! Think beyond posters or Power Point slides. Think about using props, music clips, or photographs. Some students have brought in food that related to their presentation, models to illustrate examples, and relevant film clips.

◆ Keep your audience in mind at all times. What kinds of visual aids will they respond to? Are you presenting to a technically minded audience? If so, you may want to integrate technology into your visual aid. Is your audience aesthetically motivated? Photographs, artwork, or other aesthetic media may be an effective way to reach them.

◆ Be familiar with your presentation venue, and plan according to its equipment and space limitations. Each classroom at Virginia Tech is different, and each building is equipped with its own technology. Before you make plans to use any technology, discuss the options with your teacher. Is there a projector in the room? Can you connect your own laptop to the projector? Is a key required to access the technology box? If there is no projector in your classroom and you feel that your presentation would benefit from one, discuss the options with your teacher.

◆ Be aware of the time constraints. Be mindful of the time required to set up photographs, overhead projectors, or laptop computers. Because these can be time-consuming, your teacher may limit the technology you may use, especially in the individual presentations. Arrive early on the day of your presentation so that you have time to set up equipment.

◆ When you are using visual aids that integrate text, like posters with lists or PowerPoint slides, be very aware of the size, font, and color of the text you choose. Text should be large enough to be easily seen from the back of the room, in a color that can be easily read against its background, and in a font that is clear. Limit the number of words on a visual aid; your audience cannot read more than a few concise phrases without becoming distracted from what you are saying.

9

◆ When you are working with a group, be sure to collaborate on the use of visual aids. Having one group member use a poster, another use a single PowerPoint slide, and another use no visual aid will appear inconsistent and reflect a lack of preparation and communication on the part of all group members. Communicate early and often regarding the use of visual aids in a group presentation.

◆ Always, always have a back-up plan. Technology can and often does fail. Postponing your presentation is probably not an option, so be prepared to move forward if anything and everything goes wrong. For example, you might want to have a few overhead projector transparencies prepared in case the computer fails and you can't use your PowerPoint presentation. Think ahead to what you might write or draw on the board if necessary.

◆ Be sure to integrate the visual aids into your practice. Plan when you will use and refer to them, and how you will manage your body movements to avoid obscuring your aid.

◆ Introduce your visual aid only when you are ready to refer to it. Your audience will look at whatever you place in front of them; if you are not ready to discuss information, keep it hidden. Likewise, as soon as you finish with it, remove it from the audience's view.

◆ Avoid reading directly from your visual aid. The aid is primarily for the benefit of your audience; you should be familiar with your material so that you don't need to rely on reading it.

◆ Remember your body positioning. Do not stand in front of the aid or in the path of the projector's light. If your audience is straining to see, you no longer have their full attention.

◆ Think carefully about the use of handouts. While they are easy to create and simple to use, your audience may become distracted with too much information in front of them before you are ready to refer to it.

◆ If something goes wrong with your visual aid, go to your backup plan if possible. If you cannot, just move on. We have all been in presentations when the poster fell off the wall, the projector bulb blew, or the prop malfunctioned. Your audience will take its cue from you when reacting, so apply some humor, remain calm, and proceed with your presentation.

9

9.6 Informal Writing Task: Using Your Experience To Prepare for a Successful Presentation

Step 1. Think back to some of the best and worst presentations you have seen. Think about political speeches or debates. Consider school presentations or acceptance speeches you have seen. Think back to any motivational speakers who may have visited your high school or consider some of your current teachers. Compile a list of characteristics that made a presentation either move you or lose you.

Step 2. Once you have the list, pick two or three characteristics of both successful and unsuccessful presentations and write a few sentences on why those characteristics helped or hurt the presentation.

Step 3. Once you have considered these positive and negative elements, write a paragraph about your fears or concerns. Then write down what you see as your main obstacles in delivering a presentation.

Step 4. Look at the obstacles you listed, and consider what you might do before or during the presentation to help you avoid those problems. Write a sentence or two for each one.

Once you have considered what you already know about what makes a presentation effective or ineffective, and once you've taken into account some of your fears and your specific struggles, you will be able to make some changes before the presentation that will help you make a better delivery. If you can overcome even one of your obstacles, you have succeeded in improving your communication skills.

9.7 Critical Listening

Why be an effective critical listener? Who cares? It's not your turn. You're not in the spotlight. You get to sit back and watch others sweat! What advantage is there to being a critical listener?

The truth is that if you want to be a better public speaker yourself, critical listening skills will get you there a lot faster. You are watching and listening to your classmates. Based on some of the principles presented in this chapter, what are they doing well? Where do they need improvement? When you notice how distracting it is when that young woman snaps the edges of her notecards endlessly, or that young man flips his hair over and over, or someone chews gum while speaking, you have learned what not to do by simply paying attention.

When you are impressed by a speaker's shocking statistic or vivid visual aid, you have learned about what you can do well by simply paying close attention. Witnessing another person making mistakes or succeeding is a much more powerful influence on you than just reading something like this book. You can feel the mistake like electricity in the air. You can almost hear the cheers for a job well done.

So how do you do it? What are you looking for?

Content: Consider the composition of the presentation as you might read an article or an essay. What is the speaker's main idea? How has the speaker supported that main idea? Are there enough detailed, fully-developed, and well-connected ideas to build a full picture of the issue or argument or analysis?

Form: Consider the composition of the presentation as you might experience an artistic visual and auditory composition. How is the presenter standing? Is she speaking loudly enough? Is the tone of voice appropriate to the words? Does he sound like he's reading from a script? Is the visual aid visible and available to the whole audience? Does it have a direct and obvious connection to the topic?

Because we learn from both failure and success, you will turn yourself into a more effective speaker by carefully observing others. Critical listening skills require you to use your eyes and your ears and your intellect. Through listening critically, you can give valuable feedback to your classmates, and you can learn for yourself, for the next time you speak in front of an audience.

9

Peer Review Sheet

Speaker's Name _____

Listener's Name _____

1 = **Needs Improvement**   4 = **Very Successful** _____

Comments / Suggestions

CONTENT

Introduction	1 2 3 4	
Focus	1 2 3 4	
Argument/Analysis	1 2 3 4	
Organization of Information	1 2 3 4	
Effective Use of Support	1 2 3 4	

FORM AND DELIVERY

Eye Contact	1 2 3 4	
Tone	1 2 3 4	
Volume	1 2 3 4	
Use of Hand Gestures	1 2 3 4	
Movement	1 2 3 4	

USE OF VISUAL AID

Graphic Clarity	1 2 3 4	
Incorporation	1 2 3 4	
Usefulness	1 2 3 4	

GROUP WORK (IF APPLICABLE)

Flow	1 2 3 4	
Teamwork	1 2 3 4	

Student Author Permission Form

Department of English
Virginia Tech
Blacksburg, VA 24061
540.231.6501

Pearson Education Group
75 Arlington Street, Suite #300
Boston, MA 02116
800.428.4466

I grant my permission to the Virginia Tech Department of English and to Pearson Education for reproduction and editing rights to my work submitted for this class.

ENGL _____

CRN _____

During the _____ Semester, 2005–2006.

This permission includes publication in any future edition of the English department's composition text, along with my photograph and profile —

YES _____ NO _____

— and/or publication in a collection of anonymous student work that may be used as examples in future composition classes.

YES _____ NO _____

Signature: _____

Print name: _____

Date: _____

E-mail address _____

Permanent address: _____

_____

_____